CASE CLOSED?

Nine Mysteries Unlocked
by Modern Science

Written by
Susan Hughes

Illustrated by
Michael Wandelmaier

Kids Can Press

For David Meeker, my wonderful nephew — S.H.
For Jessica — M.W.

Acknowledgments
While researching this book, I received help from many people in various countries. For their generosity in responding to my queries with detailed and expert information, and in some cases even sending photos, I would like to thank John Ashdown-Hill, David Baldwin, Carlos Bauzá, Owen Beattie, Ronald Blom, Donna Coombs, John Coombs, Jeff Dean, Jochen Hemmleb, David Jourdan, Colin and Rosemary Mudie, Tim Severin, Carlos Sorini, Richard Van Allen and Juris Zarins. Thanks as well to Russell A. Potter and Jonathon Renouf for their photos, and to illustrator Michael Wandelmaier and book designer Julia Naimska. My appreciation to the Ontario Arts Council for providing me with a grant for writing this book. In particular I would like to express my gratitude to Karen Li for bringing her editorial diligence, creativity and enthusiasm to this project.

First paperback edition 2013

Kids Can Press gratefully acknowledges the financial support of the Government of Ontario, through Ontario Creates; the Ontario Arts Council; the Canada Council for the Arts; and the Government of Canada for our publishing activity.

Published in Canada and the U.S. by Kids Can Press Ltd.
25 Dockside Drive, Toronto, ON M5A 0B5

Kids Can Press is a Corus Entertainment Inc. company

www.kidscanpress.com

Edited by Karen Li
Designed by Julia Naimska

Printed and bound in Malaysia, in 4/2019 by Tien Wah Press (Pte.) Ltd.

CM 10 0 9 8 7 6 5 4 3
CM PA 13 0 9 8 7 6 5

Library and Archives Canada Cataloguing in Publication

Hughes, Susan, 1960–
    Case closed? : nine mysteries unlocked by modern science / written by Susan Hughes ; illustrated by Michael Wandelmaier

Includes index.
ISBN 978-1-55453-362-6 (bound)
ISBN 978-1-55453-363-3 (pbk.)

1. History — Miscellanea — Juvenile literature.
2. Technological innovations — Juvenile literature.
I. Wandelmaier, Michael, 1979– II. Title.

D21.3.H84 2013   j902   C2013-901395-4

Contents

Gone Forever?

AN EXPLORER AND HIS CREW set off to the cold reaches of the Arctic Ocean in search of the Northwest Passage — and are never seen again. An airplane and its passengers are within twenty minutes of the runway — and never land. An ancient city, alive with traders and camel caravans, flourishes in the desert for centuries — and then is gone in a swirl of sand.

Over the years, stories like these have teased and tantalized the historians, archaeologists and scientists who have doggedly searched for answers. But age-old mysteries have not easily revealed their secrets ... until now.

Using both traditional search methods and modern technology, researchers around the globe are now shedding new light on old mysteries. In these pages, you'll meet the dedicated sleuths from different fields who have been seeking answers to nine disappearances, both ancient and recent. Find out which tools and techniques have been most important to each case and why. Then discover which of the vanished have been found!

Arctic Ocean

Sir John Franklin

NORTH AMERICA

The Anasazi

Atlantic Ocean

Pacific Ocean

SOUTH AMERICA

Star Dust

Arctic Ocean

★ Anastasia

EUROPE

ASIA

★ INS *Dakar*

George L. Mallory

★ Hatshepsut

★ Hsu Fu

AFRICA

★ The City of Ubar

Pacific Ocean

Indian Ocean

AUSTRALIA

Hatshepsut

IT WAS THE SPRING OF 2007. Egyptian archaeologist Dr. Zahi Hawass stood among the tombs of the Valley of the Kings in modern-day Luxor, Egypt. He took a quick breath and then turned to the rough flight of stairs cut deep into the mountain rock. Moving carefully, he began his descent into the darkness. He reached bottom and headed along a short passage.

Hawass entered the small, undecorated tomb known as KV60. The large mummy he had come to examine was stretched out on the floor. It had long hair at the back and was bald in front. Its arms were arranged in the "royal" position: one arm straight against the mummy's side; the other arm bent at the elbow, fist clenched over its chest.

Seeing it now, with his own eyes, Hawass was excited. He realized it could actually be the prize he was seeking. It could actually be the long-vanished Hatshepsut!

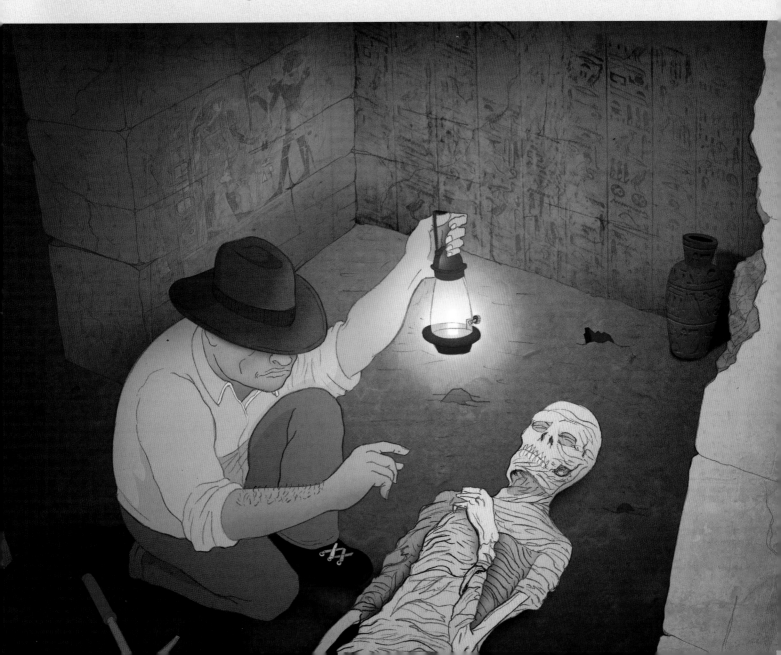

Missing: Hatshepsut — pharaoh

Date last seen: around 1457 BCE

Place last seen: Thebes, Egypt

Possible reasons for disappearance:

natural causes, murder

BACKGROUND

Hatshepsut was a powerful pharaoh who ruled Egypt about 3500 years ago. He improved Egypt's trade with peoples far and wide. He supported the arts, and Egypt prospered greatly during his reign. But there was one thing that set Hatshepsut apart from every pharaoh who had come before: "He" was a she.

Queen Hatshepsut was the daughter of King Thutmose I and wife of King Thutmose II, her half brother. But when Thutmose II died, Hatshepsut was not allowed to take the throne. In ancient Egypt, even women of royal blood could not become pharaoh. Instead, Thutmose III, Hatshepsut's stepson, was crowned. But he was too young to rule, so Hatshepsut eagerly agreed to act as regent on his behalf.

Smart and ambitious, Hatshepsut wanted power in her own right. And so she gradually made herself over as a man. She began to wear the clothing of a pharaoh, such as the kilt and false beard. She dropped all her titles that only a woman could hold. She even convinced the priests of the Temple of the Oracle to proclaim her as pharaoh. The daring strategy paid off.

Hatshepsut ruled Egypt from the royal city of Thebes for twenty-two years before Thutmose III, now a grown man, took over. And then Hatshepsut ... vanished.

Hatshepsut's fate was obscured by the fact that many signs of her were gone. Monuments were defaced. Statues of her were torn down. Her name was erased from records. And her sarcophagus, or coffin, was empty.

Some archaeologists believe Thutmose III wanted to remove evidence of the female "interruption" in the male royal lineage. By showing a clear link between Thutmose II and himself, he would make it obvious that his own son was next in line to the throne.

But how far would he have gone? Did Hatshepsut simply step down when her stepson rose to power? Or, as many historians suspect, had she been murdered by her successor? Her body might provide clues to her fate, but her official tomb in the Valley of the Kings was empty. What had become of Hatshepsut's mummy?

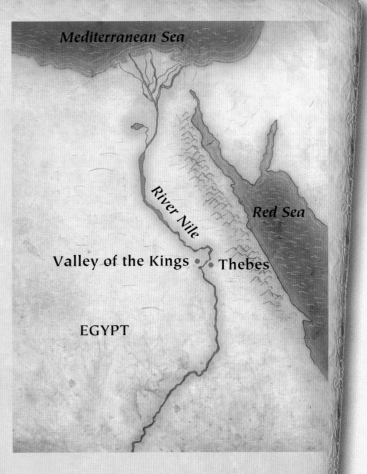

CASE OPEN

Dr. Hawass was determined to solve the mysteries of Hatshepsut's fate. He felt the answers were linked to this unknown mummy in KV60.

British archaeologist Howard Carter discovered the large mummy in 1903, alongside a sarcophagus containing the small, thin body of an elderly woman. An inscription on the sarcophagus identified the small mummy as Hatshepsut's royal wet nurse. As a result, in 1989, it was moved to the Museum of Egyptian Antiquities in Cairo. The other mummy was left behind, of little interest.

Hawass thought this mummy might be Hatshepsut herself. He arranged to have the large mummy transported to the Cairo museum. He wanted computerized axial tomography (CAT) scans done of both of the KV60 mummies, along with several other unidentified mummies.

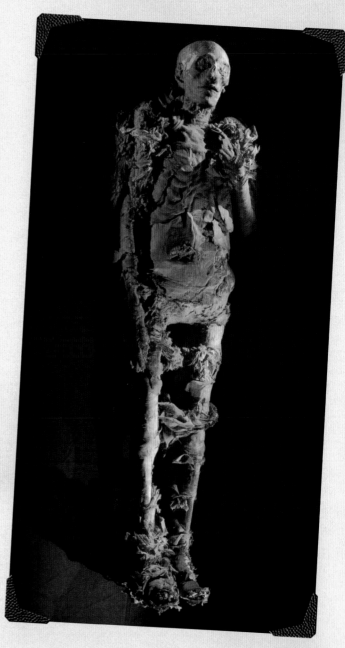

Mixed-up Mummies

In ancient Egypt, priests were sometimes worried about thieves breaking into the royal tombs to loot them. They moved some mummies from their original tombs and hid them in other tombs to protect their bodies. When a mummy has been moved, archaeologists have a more difficult time identifying it because they cannot use surrounding objects as clues.

Hatshepsut's original tomb, known as Deir el-Bahri, was an architectural masterpiece: Three pillared terraces were built deep into a rock face, accessible by two long ramps. But Hatshepsut was not buried there. The tomb was empty, and so was her sarcophagus.

In 1903, archaeologist Howard Carter discovered the large mummy shown in this photograph. In 2007, Dr. Zawi Hawass came to examine the mummy. He hoped that new scientific technology could help solve the mystery of the mummy's identity.

Looking at a CAT scan lets people see inside a body the way looking at a slice of bread lets you see inside the loaf. A CAT scan uses computers and revolving X-rays to create cross-sectioned views or three-dimensional computer models of a body's internal organs and structures.

CAT scanning could be done without touching or damaging the fragile mummies. Hawass hoped the scans would reveal whether one of the mummies was Hatshepsut and what might have caused her death.

Doctors use CAT scans to help identify medical diseases, such as cancer and heart disease. It lets them see inside the human body without having to perform surgery. The CAT scans provide images in high resolution. Tiny tumors that would not show up on an X-ray can be seen on a CAT scan.

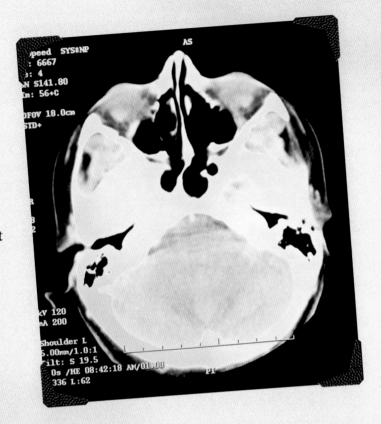

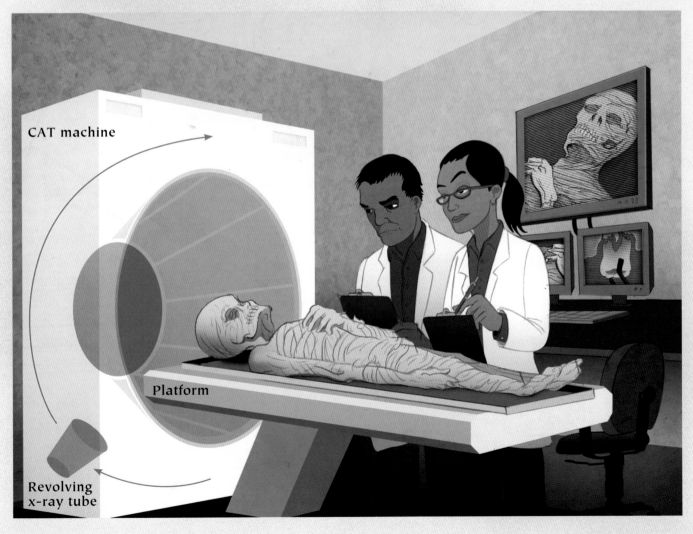

CAT machine

Platform

Revolving
x-ray tube

Mistaken Identity

Researchers also scanned some other mummies that had been found in tomb DB320. They were surprised to find that the mummy they'd believed was Thutmose I was not that of Hatshepsut's elderly father. Instead, CAT scans revealed a forty-year-old man with an arrow embedded in his chest. A new mystery now begs to be solved: Where is Thutmose I?

Researchers conducted CAT scans of four female mummies in total. Two were from KV60 and two others were from another tomb called DB320.

Tomb DB320 was about 1 km (0.6 mi.) from KV60. It contained forty royal mummies, some of them unidentified. It also contained a small box, found in 1881. The box was inscribed with Hatshepsut's royal seal. Because this box had been found in DB320, Hawass figured that Hatshepsut's mummy might have been moved there, too. Possibly, it was one of two mummies taken from DB320 and stored in the Museum of Egyptian Antiquities and now being CAT scanned.

The physicians examined the CAT scans of all four female mummies. Although the scans revealed intriguing details about each mummy, they could not positively identify Hatshepsut. Doggedly, Hawass continued his search.

Late one night, after the body scans had been completed, Hawass began thinking about the small wooden box of DB320. When mummies are embalmed, their internal organs are taken out, preserved and stored in sacred jars and boxes. Hawass wondered if something inside Hatshepsut's box might provide a clue to her whereabouts. He decided to have the box scanned, too.

The CAT scan revealed a liver, an intestine … and something much more thrilling — a broken tooth. Hawass was extremely excited because teeth are as unique as fingerprints. What if he could match Hatshepsut's tooth to one of the mummies' jaws?

Right away, a professor of orthodontics from Cairo University was called in to help. He studied all the CAT scans and discovered that the larger mummy from KV60 was missing the same type of tooth as the one found in the box — a molar. The dentist did some measurements and concluded that the broken tooth fit within a fraction of a millimeter into the mummy's upper jaw socket. It was a match!

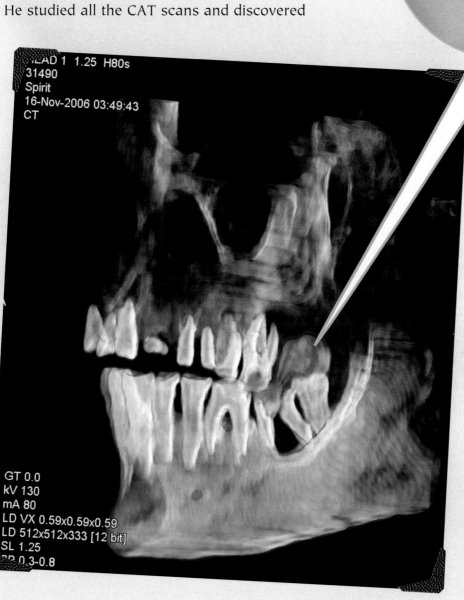

HEAD 1 1.25 H80s
31490
Spirit
16-Nov-2006 03:49:43
CT

GT 0.0
kV 130
mA 80
LD VX 0.59x0.59x0.59
LD 512x512x333 [12 bit]
SL 1.25
RB 0.3-0.8

This CAT scan, taken on November 16, 2006, shows the empty socket in the jaw of the large mummy from tomb KV60. The tooth found in the box was almost a perfect match. Also, scientists measured the density of the molar found in the box and compared it to the densities of the mummy's teeth. The results? Nearly identical densities, and more proof that the molar is from the large mummy's jaw.

MYSTERY SOLVED?

After centuries of mystery and speculation, it seems Hatshepsut's mummy has been found. The first round of DNA testing has matched the large mummy's DNA to that of Ahmose Nefertari, Hatshepsut's grandmother.

But did the body reveal whether or not the female pharaoh had been murdered? Looking at the mummy's CAT scan, researchers agreed that the woman had died between the ages of forty-five and sixty. She had major dental problems and was overweight. She may have had diabetes.

The verdict? Physicians saw evidence that Hatshepsut may have died of cancer. There was no sign that foul play had caused her death.

CASE CLOSED

... But where is the mummy of Hatshepsut's father, King Thutmose I?

A carving of a pharaoh (left), perhaps with the ancient-Egyptian god Amun, sits unfinished in Hatshepsut's temple, Deir el-Bahri, near modern-day Luxor. In many places in her own temple, Hatshepsut's name has been replaced with the name of Thutmose III. Many engravings showing Hatshepsut have been destroyed.

Hsu Fu

IT WAS MID-MAY 1993. Standing aboard the raft, Tim Severin took one last look at the Hong Kong shore. He and his crew were about to begin a dangerous experiment: to see if it was possible to cross the Pacific Ocean on an ancient-style vessel — a raft 18 m (60 ft.) long and made entirely of bamboo and rattan.

Severin didn't pause. He gave the signal to untie the lines. Then he turned his back on land and faced the sea. The *Hsu Fu* set sail.

What drove the Irish explorer to set out on such a quest? He was inspired by the voyage of another man with a similar thirst for adventure. A man after whom he had named his raft. A man who had vanished long ago.

Missing: Hsu Fu — explorer, monk, mariner

Date last seen: around 215 BCE

Place last seen: China

Possible reasons for disappearance: drowned at sea, settled in Japan, sailed to America

BACKGROUND

Over two thousand years ago, a Buddhist monk named Hsu Fu was called to the court of the first emperor of China, Shih Huang Ti. The emperor told Hsu Fu of a miraculous plant that could bring eternal life. The plant could be found on three legendary islands, known as Pheng Lai, Fang Zhang and Ying Zhou. The emperor was sending Hsu Fu to fetch the plant because the monk was also an accomplished explorer and navigator.

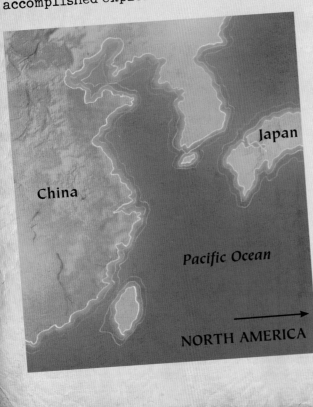

Several years went by. The emperor heard nothing from Hsu Fu. Suddenly, Hsu Fu reappeared one day. He reported that he had met a sea magician and a dragon near one of the three islands. They had asked for offerings: 3000 young men and women, as well as workers of all trades. The emperor agreed to provide these sacrifices. Hsu Fu set sail again, with people and supplies on board.

Emperor Shih Huang Ti died in 210 BCE, waiting in vain for the life-sustaining plant. Hsu Fu never returned to China. One legend says that he reached Japan, where he settled and made himself a king. Another says he sailed as far as America.

But how far across the ocean could Hsu Fu have possibly ventured on an ancient Chinese vessel? Could he truly have sailed to Japan, or even all the way across the Pacific Ocean to America?

CASE OPEN

Tim Severin decided to make the journey himself. If he could cross from Asia to America on an ancient-style vessel, he could argue that the Chinese may have traveled to the Americas long before Columbus.

First, Severin had to figure out what type of boat Hsu Fu would have used for such an ambitious journey. Severin met with marine historians. He traveled to Taiwan and then Vietnam to take a look at some traditional boats. He decided that Hsu Fu's boat was probably a sailing raft made of bamboo. These workhorse vessels had been used for centuries by local fishermen along the coast. They were sturdy and reliable — for short distances, anyway.

Hsu Fu would have needed something larger than a fishing boat to tackle the ocean. But what would it have looked like? Severin asked British naval engineer Colin Mudie to design a vessel based on Severin's research.

Mudie's final sketch showed a boat that would be 18 m (60 ft.) long. Three layers of bamboo would keep it stable in high waves. And two thatched "cabins" would give the crew some protection from the elements.

When it was time to build the real thing, Severin hired Vietnamese village women who were experts in harvesting bamboo. In the middle of the jungle, they found a species of bamboo with stalks 9 m (30 ft.) tall and 15 cm (6 in.) wide. They harvested two-year-old stalks, which are still flexible, and they harvested them in autumn, when the stalks produce little sap. (Bamboo sap attracts the bamboo beetle, whose larvae eat plant matter.)

In the Vietnamese fishing village of Sam Son, forty raft builders used machetes to shave away the hard outer layer of the bamboo stalks. They curved the stalks at the bow by heating them just so with flames. Then they coated the 350 stalks with a natural repellent to keep away the insects and a natural lacquer to protect them from shipworm infection. The stalks were lashed together with rattan, a type of jungle vine. They used 46 km (29 mi.) of it, tying more than 3000 knots. The raft builders fitted the raft with three cedar masts, red sails of cotton and silk, and several very long oars.

Bamboo beetle

Why Bamboo?

Pros: Bamboo floats because it has thin walls and large internal air chambers. Bamboo stalks will flex with the waves and so avoid being ripped apart by them.

Cons: Bamboo attracts sap-eating insects if it is not harvested at the right time of year. Bamboo can be chewed to pieces by shipworm while at sea.

Shipworm

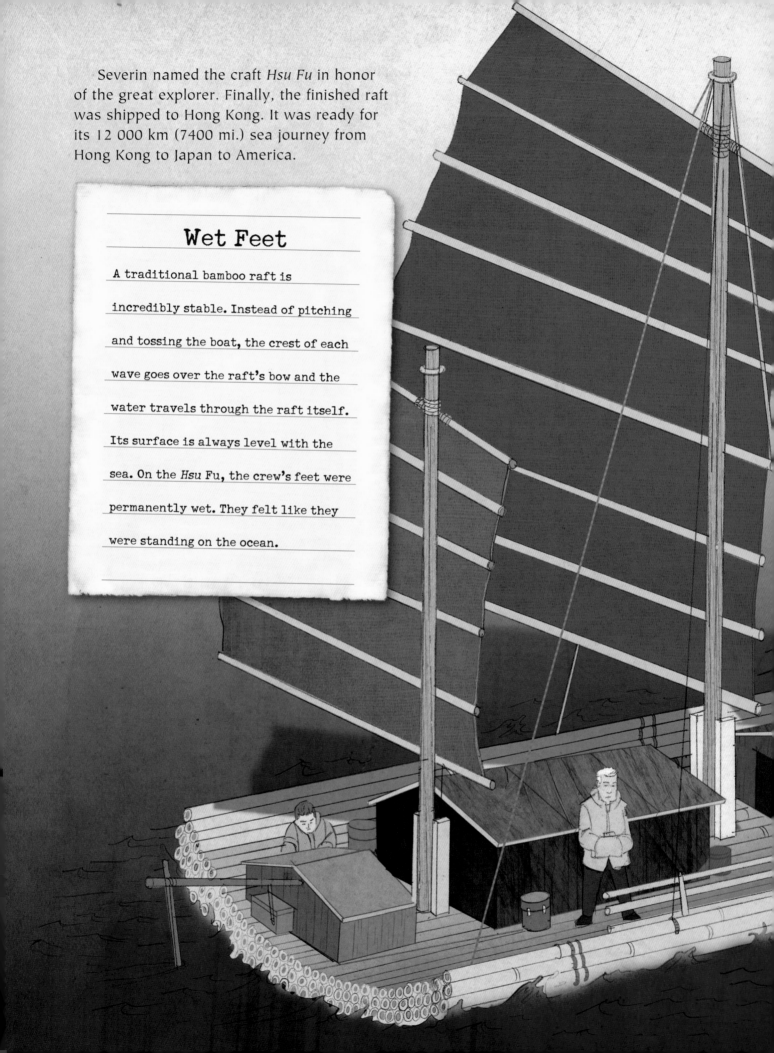

Severin named the craft *Hsu Fu* in honor of the great explorer. Finally, the finished raft was shipped to Hong Kong. It was ready for its 12 000 km (7400 mi.) sea journey from Hong Kong to Japan to America.

Wet Feet

A traditional bamboo raft is incredibly stable. Instead of pitching and tossing the boat, the crest of each wave goes over the raft's bow and the water travels through the raft itself. Its surface is always level with the sea. On the *Hsu* Fu, the crew's feet were permanently wet. They felt like they were standing on the ocean.

The ancient Chinese were expert astronomers. They were one of the first peoples to navigate by the sun and stars. By 350 BCE, 140 or years or so before Hsu Fu set off on his journey, Chinese astronomers had created one of the world's earliest star catalogues, containing 120 entries. The earliest Chinese book on sea navigation was written during the Han dynasty (202 BCE to 220 CE), which explains how to find north by locating the polar star.

Severin decided to navigate as the ancient Chinese would have done. He tried to follow the general route he believed Hsu Fu would have taken. "But this was no more than trying to head in an easterly direction. We were riding wind and current," he said.

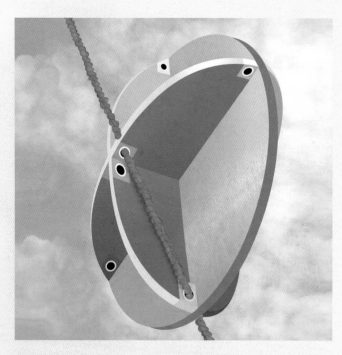

To protect themselves from being run down by large ships, crew members hoisted a radar reflector in stormy or foggy conditions. A radar reflector is made of sheet metal with many reflective surfaces. When a ship's radar beam hit the reflector, it would bounce back, alerting the ship's crew to the presence of the raft. Large ships use metal-detecting radar to spot objects on the water. Without the radar reflector, the small, nonmetallic raft would have been undetectable in bad weather.

Some modern inventions that Severin brought aboard included a satellite radio. Its battery was charged by a small windmill or solar panels. He could use it to send written communications to anywhere in the world — essential in case of an emergency. Also aboard were flares, a survival suit for each crew member and a lifeboat. In addition, the *Hsu Fu* carried a standard Emergency Position Indicating Radio Beacon, which could quickly identify the tiny craft's position by sending out a digital distress signal to be picked up by satellite.

The journey began well, but within a few days, Severin saw signs that the bamboo beetle was chewing away the cabin roofs. He desperately hoped the beetles would not make their way into the raft itself.

In the meantime, the crew worked hard. The waves caused great twisting and straining of the raft. At various points in the journey, this caused parts of the boat, including the rattan and the ropes, to wear. In fact, off Japan's Ryukyu Islands, the foremast snapped off. The crew replaced it with a shaved-down telegraph pole, which, although not traditional, was "the only long straight timber on the island," explained Severin.

Fifty-six days and 2900 km (1800 mi.) later, the raft arrived at its first destination — Shingu, Japan. One mystery had now been answered: Hsu Fu certainly could have made it to Japan by raft 2200 years ago.

The local people of Shingu had long been certain he had. They showed Severin a shrine to Hsu Fu at the site of his supposed grave. Some people believe Hsu Fu brought new farming techniques and plants to Japan, including rice cultivation. Some Japanese worship him as an ancestor; some worship Hsu Fu as a god of farming or god of medicine.

Tim Severin checking rotten fastenings on Hsu Fu.

A crew member replaces rotting mast stays on Hsu Fu.

In early August, Severin and his crew prepared to tease out the answer to the next part of the puzzle: Could Hsu Fu have continued on across the Pacific to America? Could he have made it on a bamboo vessel? The expedition set sail from Japan. The real test — open water as far as the eye could see — began.

The raft sailed on and was fairly problem free for months, although the crew was always busy with repairs. Then in early November, when the *Hsu Fu* was 3200 km (2000 mi.) off the coast of North America, there were signs of real trouble. The rattan was beginning to dissolve. Some of the bamboo stalks in the hull were coming loose. Then, 1600 km (1000 mi.) from the North American coast, several stalks actually drifted away. Shipworm was eating the bamboo. The raft was deteriorating. It was losing its buoyancy, sinking deeper and deeper into the ocean.

Severin made a difficult decision, one

that Hsu Fu could not have made 2200 years ago: He had to evacuate the raft: "I sent a message via Sat-C link, similar to a modern text message, to my shore contact at the Mariner's Museum in Newport News, Virginia." A passing container ship was alerted to their danger and picked them up. The journey was over.

ASIA

NORTH AMERICA

Hsu Fu's Route

Pacific Ocean

MYSTERY SOLVED?

Despite his raft's failure to make it all the way to America, Severin considers his trip a success. The experiment provided evidence that Hsu Fu could have made the dangerous trans-Pacific journey in a raft 2200 years ago.

According to Severin, "Our own experiment showed the seaworthiness of the raft we used. If I had insisted on coating the rattan fastenings with pitch/tar, the structure would have survived to complete the voyage. Given that the original Chinese mission deployed a large number of rafts, it is reasonable to assume that some of them would have completed the trans-oceanic voyage."

Tim Severin, standing, and the crew of the Hsu Fu sail on the Pacific Ocean toward North America. Their historic voyage in 1993 was an attempt to determine whether the ancient Chinese could have traveled to the Americas over two thousand years ago.

THE INVESTIGATION CONTINUES

... Is there any proof that the Chinese landed in the Americas before Columbus?

The City of Ubar

RONALD BLOM WAS SITTING AT HIS DESK at NASA's Jet Propulsion Laboratory (JPL). It was 1983. On the scientist's computer monitor was a note: "Dare to be stupid!"

The phone rang. Blom picked it up to hear a hesitant voice say, "I would like to talk to someone about using the Space Shuttle to look for a lost city."

A lost city? Blom's interest was tweaked. He arranged to meet the caller, filmmaker Nicholas Clapp, for lunch that same day. Blom says, "I just had to hear more about this unusual quest."

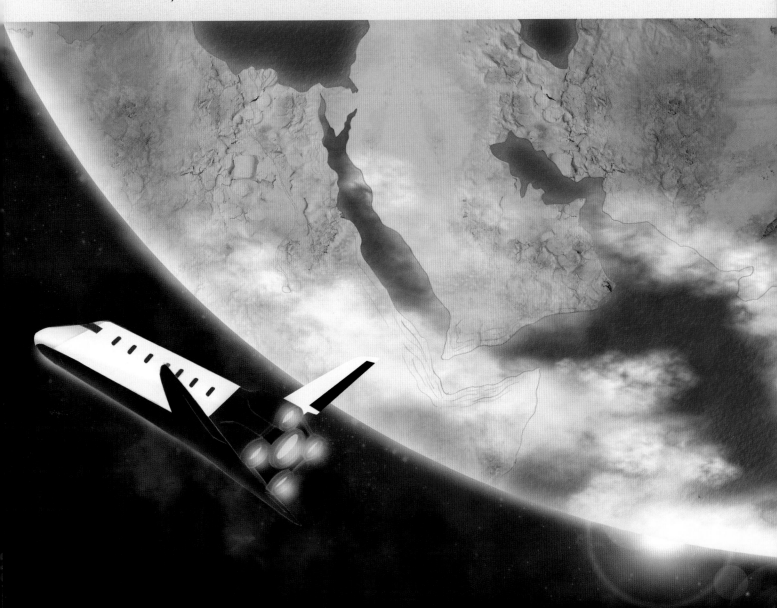

Missing: Ubar — city

Date last seen: around 300 CE

Place last seen: Rub' al-Khali desert in the Arabian Peninsula

Possible reasons for disappearance: destroyed by God's vengeance, destroyed by a great wind or hurricane

BACKGROUND

Legend tells us of a remarkable city called Ubar that came into existence about 5000 years ago. It stood in the great Rub' al-Khali desert in the southern part of the Arabian Peninsula. It had vast groves of fruit trees and breathtaking architecture. Its citizens were rich, for Ubar was a wealthy hub on a well-traveled trade route.

Frankincense trees grew in the valley nearby. The aromatic resin from the trees was used for many purposes, from making incense for religious ceremonies to embalming corpses. Caravans of thousands of camels came and went from Ubar to pick up the precious frankincense and deliver it to destinations as distant as Rome and China.

But around 300 CE, after flourishing for thousands of years, Ubar seemed to simply vanish.

Rashid al-Din, a thirteenth-century historian, wrote that Ubar was ruled by an arrogant and sinful king named Shaddad, son of Ad and grandson of Noah. The king and his people ignored a prophet's warning to change their wicked ways. God punished them, destroying the city with a huge wind and overrunning it with evil creatures.

Did the city of Ubar ever really exist? If so, why were scholars and explorers unable to locate its ruins?

ARABIAN PENINSULA

Rub' al-Khali Desert

Arabian Sea

CASE OPEN

In 1980, Nicholas Clapp first heard of the elusive lost city — and began to dream of discovering it. He read voraciously, trying to find clues about where Ubar might be. He learned that in 1930, Bertram Thomas, the first European to cross the Rub' al-Khali desert, had found the well-worn tracks of an ancient caravan route. His Bedouin guide told him it was "the road to Ubar."

Clapp dug deeper in the Koran, in writings by Greek and Roman historians, and in works by Islamic geographers. In the early thirteenth century, historian Yaqut ibn-'Abdallah's *Dictionary of Lands* described the City of Wabar (or Ubar) as a great oasis with a large population and "a big well called the Well of Wabar."

Clapp pored over an original map of the area created by Claudius Ptolemy, an ancient geographer and astronomer. He compared it with a centuries-old reproduction of Ptolemy's map. Both maps showed a region marked Iobaritae (Latin for "land of the Ubarites") but no city in the region. However, both maps also showed a major settlement called Omanum Emporium ("a market town of Oman") in western Arabia at 87° latitude. Oddly, in the reproduction map's table of coordinates, the town was listed at 78° latitude. Eighty-seven. Seventy-eight. Was it possible the numbers had been reversed by mistake on the original map? Could the reproduction have corrected the error?

Excited, Clapp traced 78° latitude on the map to eastern Arabia, right above Iobaritae. At 78° latitude, the market town was out in the desert, just north of Thurifera regio, or "Incense Land." This location, so close to the groves where frankincense trees grew, would have been the perfect place from which to market the valuable plant.

Claudius Ptolemy was born in Egypt at the end of the first century CE. He used manuscripts and trading records of coastlines to create a map of the world, complete with longitude and latitude.

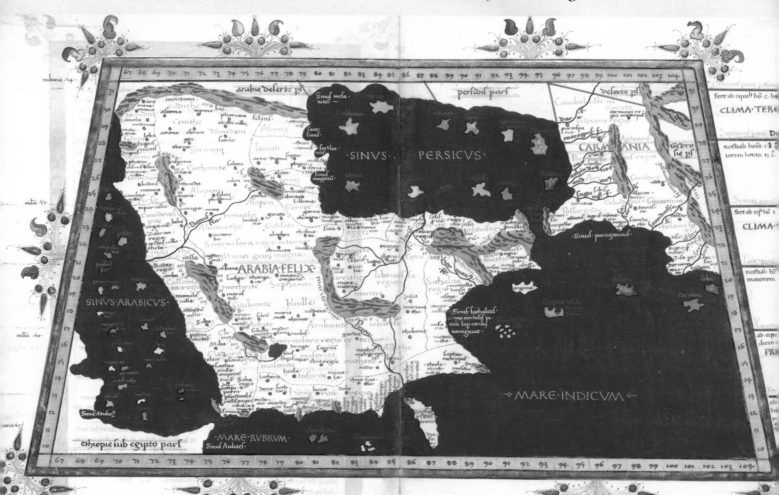

Clapp was now ready to bring in some twentieth-century technology. That's when he made the call to Ronald Blom at NASA's Jet Propulsion Laboratory. Clapp knew the *Challenger* space shuttle had been making radar images of Earth on its orbits. He suggested to Blom that they use the shuttle's radar to look for signs of the lost city from space.

In October 1984, *Challenger* blasted off with the Shuttle Imaging Radar-B (SIR-B) aboard. As the shuttle flew over Earth, it beamed pulses of microwave energy toward several sites, including, with Blom's go-ahead, Arabia. The pulses could travel through clouds, vegetation and even penetrate up to 2 m (7 ft.) into the desert sand. The signals that bounced back were converted into radar images.

When Clapp and Blom looked at the images of Arabia, they were surprised to see evidence of ancient streams and rivers. Water had once run through this part of the desert! But there was no sign of the road to Ubar or the city itself.

The Space Shuttle Challenger *(above) launches on an early October morning in 1984. The dark launch complex is illuminated by spotlights as* Challenger *begins its ascent from the pad.*

The SIR-B can give information about the texture of materials. For example, rocks, which are rough, show up bright on a radar image, while sand, which is smooth, shows up dark.

Blom suggested that satellite shots of the area might be more helpful. The Landsat 5 satellite was equipped with an instrument called a Thematic Mapper. "The instrument is very, very good at discriminating amongst materials," says Blom.

An artist's depiction of the Landsat 7 satellite, the next generation of the Landsat technology used to find the lost city of Ubar. Onboard, the Enhanced Thematic Mapper Plus (ETM +) is like the highly successful Thematic Mapper instrument on Landsat 5.

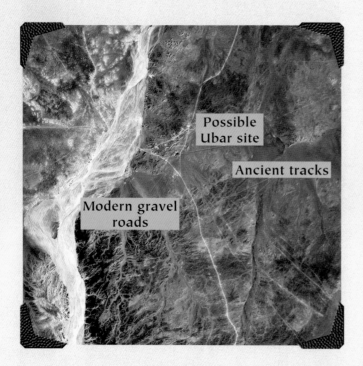

Possible Ubar site

Ancient tracks

Modern gravel roads

If the SIR-B was somewhat like an X-ray, the Thematic Mapper was somewhat like a camera. Blom and Clapp hoped it could show them more details about the surface material of Arabia. The Thematic Mapper detected the electromagnetic energy from objects on land. It could pick up three types of light spectrums: the visible spectrum, the infrared spectrum and the thermal spectrum. Also, it could "see" a large area in a single scene — over 30 0000 square km (12 000 square mi.).

In 1986, the Landsat 5 satellite passed over the area where Clapp hoped to find Ubar. The Thematic Mapper created an image, and Clapp and Blom were amazed to see thin lines where the earth had been compressed over thousands of years into rows and rows of tracks. It had to be the road to Ubar. And just where Bertram Thomas had seen it!

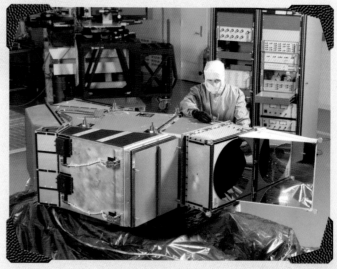

A NASA engineer (above) with the Landsat 7 ETM + instrument.

Objects reflect different amounts of electromagnetic radiation at different wavelengths. Viewed by a Thematic Mapper, old leaves, for example, will show different hues of green than new ones.

This photo (left) was taken by the Thematic Mapper on the Landsat 5 satellite. A dry streambed runs across the image as a thick white line. Pinkish streaks show ancient tracks to Ubar.

Encouraged, Clapp and his research team, including Blom and archaeologist Juris Zarins, headed to Arabia to study the area in the summer of 1990. From Salalah, Oman, they flew out over the desert by helicopter. From the air, they could see parts of the road to Ubar, but after landing, they realized it was almost invisible from the ground. No wonder earlier explorers had experienced such difficulties finding the road!

The team also landed for a short visit in a small village called Shisur. Wandering through its ruined fort, Zarins recognized artifacts that were quite old — perhaps as old as Ubar. "Juris was in fact suspicious," recalls Blom. But the team did not have much information on Shisur, and it was not among their space images.

An Expert Opinion

Blom says, "There are lots of things to be discovered out there, and there are many new tools that can help one in these kinds of searches. It's important to use experts from many different fields. When searching for Ubar, we had an historian, an archaeologist, a documentary movie producer and a space cadet — me! — and it would not have worked without all of us. None of us could have done it on our own."

Recon over, the research team headed home to the United States. Over the next eighteen months, they gathered more images, including many of Shisur. Roads, both old and new, came and went from there. They began to believe that the village, a small oasis in the desert, was a key site in the area. Could it be Ubar?

With renewed optimism, Clapp and the team returned to Oman in 1991. Their targets? The roads to Ubar and Shisur.

They visited with the Shahra people, who still trade in incense. They saw the nearby frankincense groves and the ancient cave art of the People of 'Ad. Then the team headed into the desert by Land Rover. They carried radios, compasses and a global positioning system (GPS), hoping the equipment would help them intercept the road to Ubar. For five days, they hunted through the dunes. They followed many tracks, but found no sign of the lost city.

Disappointed, the team headed next to Shisur to explore its ruined fort, built in the 1500s. They were examining its tower when Zarins noticed that the stonework at the top of the tower was different than at the bottom. Was the tower older than it seemed? The team was also intrigued by a sinkhole at the edge of town. It looked as though it had been caused by the collapse of an underground cavern. Was it possible that the "great wind" that had caused Ubar to sink into the sands had also caused this cavern to collapse?

To be Ubar, Shisur would have to be over 1500 years old. The team needed to look for clues beneath sands that had built up over hundreds of years. To do that, they again used radar. This time, the team dragged ground-penetrating radar equipment, called "the red sled," over the sinkhole area. It sent and received radar signals, and scribbled a rough image of what lay beneath. The team saw solid rock almost 10 m (30 ft.) down. Then, recalls Blom, "the red sled revealed the remains of what we thought might be a well in the bottom of the sinkhole." But this still didn't date the site for them.

The team, helped by volunteers, began digging at the site. They uncovered broken walls of three small rooms on a ridge running east from the old fort. As the days went by, they found hundreds of pottery shards — the oldest over 1600 years. Excitement began to build, especially when they found the stone foundation of what had once been a wall, running along the ridge. In the third week of digging, they found one tower and then another.

By the end of the fifth week, seven towers and more of the fortress wall had been found, plus the outlines of shops backing onto the encircling walls. The diggers had uncovered many more artifacts, including pieces of one of the oldest chess sets in the world (750 CE to 850 CE). Clearly, the site was ancient.

One of the group's guides stands by a frankincense tree.

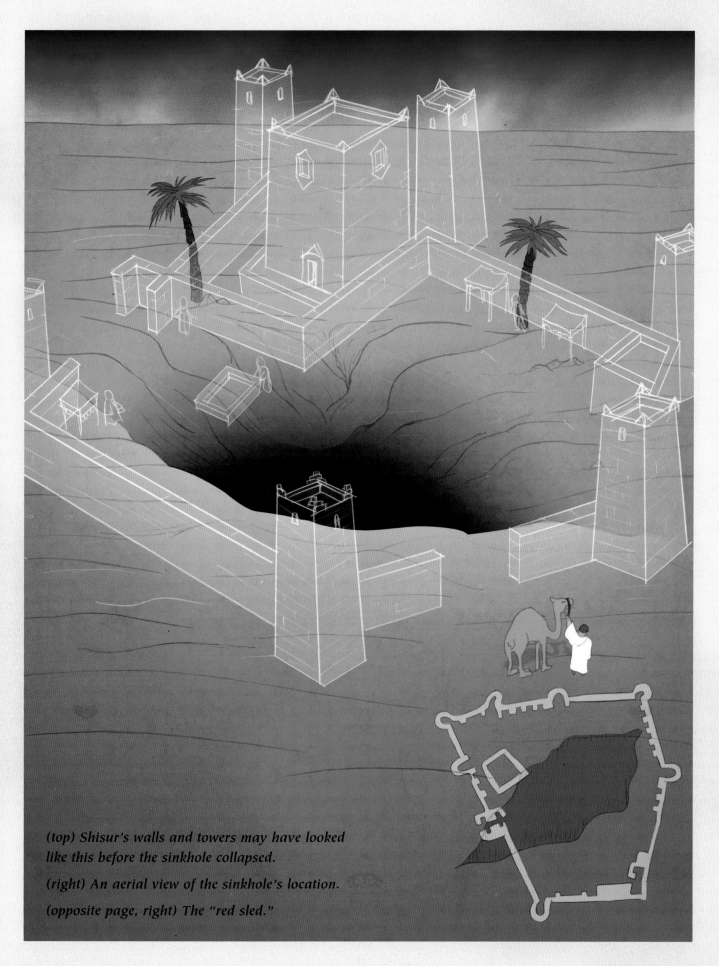

(top) Shisur's walls and towers may have looked like this before the sinkhole collapsed.

(right) An aerial view of the sinkhole's location.

(opposite page, right) The "red sled."

MYSTERY SOLVED?

Had the team found Ubar? Clapp looked at the facts. The underground fortress matched many of the features mentioned in old legends and in the Koran: Like Ubar, this ancient city was built in a remote and desolate area of Arabia. Its towers made it a "city of lofty buildings," as Ubar was described in the Koran. Its water source, now a sinkhole, could be the "well of Wabar."

In addition, it appeared that after 300 CE, the limestone on which the fortress rested gave way, perhaps because of a distant earthquake. Half of the structure split off, plunging into the underground cavern. This was when Ubar "sank into the sands."

The team in modern-day Oman, searching the Rub' al-Khali desert for the lost city of Ubar: Nicholas Clapp (second from the left), Ronald Blom (sitting center front with hat), Juris Zarins (far right).

It all added up, like pieces of a puzzle snapping into place. The seekers of the lost city agreed: Ubar may not have been a city at all. In fact, it was most likely a fort surrounding a well. But its importance was unquestionable. It was a key location where camel caravans carrying frankincense assembled. As Blom points out, "It became a 'city' in legend."

CASE CLOSED

... But are there other archaeological treasures to be found along the ancient caravan route?

The Anasazi

JEFFREY DEAN, ARCHAEOLOGIST and professor at the University of Arizona, stared at the computer screen. He was about to watch history come to life. Onscreen, he saw the Four Corners region of the United States (modern-day Colorado, Arizona, New Mexico and Utah) as it existed in the thirteenth century.

Everything looked about right. Dean had provided data about the climate and the landscape of the time. Other archaeologists had supplied information about the crops grown and tools used. And — although they were simulations — the "people," or agents onscreen were programmed to act reasonably in response to their changing environment.

The computer program started, and the clock began ticking. Time advanced from 800 CE, and Dean watched as crops were planted, the population grew and villages increased in size. The date kept scrolling forward. Now Dean held his breath. What would happen when it reached 1300? Would the people simply up and vanish like the real Anasazi had done over 700 years ago?

Missing: the Anasazi — ancient Pueblo peoples

Date last seen: around 1300

Place last seen: southwestern North America

Possible reasons for disappearance: war, drought, starvation

BACKGROUND

The Anasazi (an-a-SAH-zee) had been an ancient nomadic people. For 10 000 years, they lived by hunting wild deer and gathering fruit, wild berries, nuts and other wild plants.

About 1800 years ago, they began settling in the plateau region of southwestern America, where sources of water and good farmland could be found. They built single-storey adobe shelters with wood, mortar and sandstone, and began living in villages, called pueblos. They grew crops and domesticated wild turkeys and dogs.

Rapidly, the population grew. The people gathered in larger pueblos within the canyons. They built dams, canals, reservoirs and even an observatory high atop Chimney Rock, in what is now southwestern Colorado. They used their remarkable building skills to construct multistoried "great houses," similar to modern apartment blocks, with mortar and huge logs transported from mountain-tops over 100 km (60 mi.) away. Some of these great houses had over 600 rooms and housed over 1000 people.

The Anasazi wove cotton clothing and blankets. They created art images on rock, perhaps to share important messages. They marked the passing of time so they would know when to plant their crops or harvest them. Spurred on by surplus crops, such as beans, squash and cotton, the Anasazi developed extensive trade routes. Hundreds of kilometers (miles) of roads connected more than seventy outside communities to Chaco Canyon, likely the center of the Anasazi civilization.

But suddenly, about 1300 CE, the Anasazi left their homes and vanished! Where did they go?

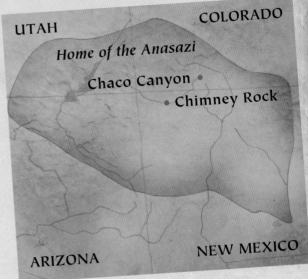

The Anasazi people lived here, where the current states of Utah, Colorado, New Mexico and Arizona meet.

Cliff Palace, an ancient Anasazi dwelling, is part of Mesa Verde National Park in Southwestern Colorado.

CASE OPEN

When the Anasazi people "vanished," so did the stories, legends or traditions that might have given us pointers to their past. Anthropologists, who study how human cultures develop, had to turn to other peoples in the region for clues about the Anasazi. They discovered that most of the modern Pueblo peoples of Arizona and New Mexico, including the Hopi and the Zuni, count the Anasazi among their ancestors.

Archaeologists, such as Jeffery Dean, support this idea. Ancient artifacts show us that areas to the south of Chaco Canyon became more and more crowded at the time that the Anasazi "disappeared," making archaeologists think that the Anasazi actually moved south. Dean says, "Virtually all archaeologists agree that the Anasazi didn't really vanish." But what could have caused every person to pack up and abandon cities that had flourished for hundreds of years?

Vanished Names

We do not know what the Anasazi called themselves. The Navajo called them anasazi, which means "ancient people who are not us" or "enemy ancestors." Some modern Pueblo people, such as the Hopi, find this offensive. They call their ancestors the Hisatsinom, which means "people of long ago."

38

Archaeologists analyzed human bones from the 1300s found in the area. Some showed evidence of famine and malnutrition. Many infants died. Were these signs that food had become scarce? The Anasazi lived about 2100 m (6900 ft.) above sea level, where precipitation and the growing season were good for farming. But if the weather had changed dramatically, the Anasazi — who relied on crops for their survival — may have been forced to evacuate.

To know more about the history of precipitation in the area, researchers turned to dendrochronology, which is the study and dating of tree rings. A tree usually grows a new ring every year. The width of the ring is mainly affected by how much water and warmth the tree experienced. Dry years produce narrow rings, and wet years produce wide rings.

Scientists take a core sample from a tree and examine it. They try to match each ring to its corresponding calendar year. Then they can examine a ring's width and learn about what the environment was like that year. They might be able to tell, for example, how much rain fell, what the temperature was and even whether there was an insect outbreak.

Dean analyzed tree rings in the region. He found that in 1250, weather patterns became chaotic and unpredictable. He says, "Farming could no longer support the number of people that lived in the area. This, of course, increased competition for dwindling resources. In some areas, this resulted in Anasazi communities fighting with each other."

Tree Ring-ologies

Scientists study tree rings to learn about many things, such as

- climatology (for example, past dry spells or cold periods);
- ecology (for example, past insect epidemics or forest fires);
- geology (for example, past volcanic eruptions or earthquakes); and
- anthropology (for example, past construction or desertion of societies).

Dating tree rings isn't as easy as counting backwards from the bark. Sometimes bands are absent. This can happen when insects strip the leaves from one part of a tree. Other times, there might be false bands. These can occur during dry spells. So to accurately pair tree rings with calendar years, dendrochronologists have to carefully match patterns in ring widths from tree to tree. They compare new samples to verified samples to spot absent or false bands.

Other evidence supports Dean's theory. Archaeologists have discovered that in the 1200s, some Anasazi people began moving to higher ground, building pueblos into shallow caves in the cliff walls. Archaeologists think that one of the reasons the Anasazi moved into these "cliff dwellings" was because they offered protection from enemies.

And if famine and warfare weren't enough to drive away the Anasazi, some archaeologists offer another factor: religion. The Anasazi depended on predictable rainfall patterns for their crops, so they might have felt spiritual connections with nature. When the weather worsened, the people might have felt that connection was broken. To the Anasazi society, this spiritual break — in combination with conflict and drought — could have been catastrophic.

Archaeologists have found signs of spiritual upheaval in other societies in the region. Perhaps a new type of religion, formed to the south, had appealed to the Anasazi people. This could have triggered the Anasazi to pick up and join a community with a more attractive faith.

Dean was excited to take part in another attempt to shed some light on the mystery. He and several other archaeologists, a social scientist and a computer modeler created the Artificial Anasazi Project. The simulation program constructed an artificial Anasazi society. Specifically, it showed how the people living in Long House Valley — an actual Anasazi settlement — might have behaved from 800 CE to 1350 CE. The model used 3-D satellite maps of the area and recreated known environmental factors, such as climate, crop production and drought.

The simulation was "agent based," which means that each person who lived in the historical Anasazi settlement was represented by an agent. The agents were programmed so that they would act in simple, reasonable ways in response to events and conditions.

When the researchers ran the program, they watched with great interest as the date advanced. By the time 1300 CE rolled around, three-quarters of the Anasazi agents had left the valley. But some remained.

Major Motions

Many computer programs try to simulate models of a natural system. One example is weather forecasting. Artists also use a technology known as swarm intelligence to simulate realistic crowds of people or animals. For example, the technology helped them create the movement of a group of penguins in the movie *Batman Returns* and show large-scale movements during battle scenes in the Lord of the Rings movies.

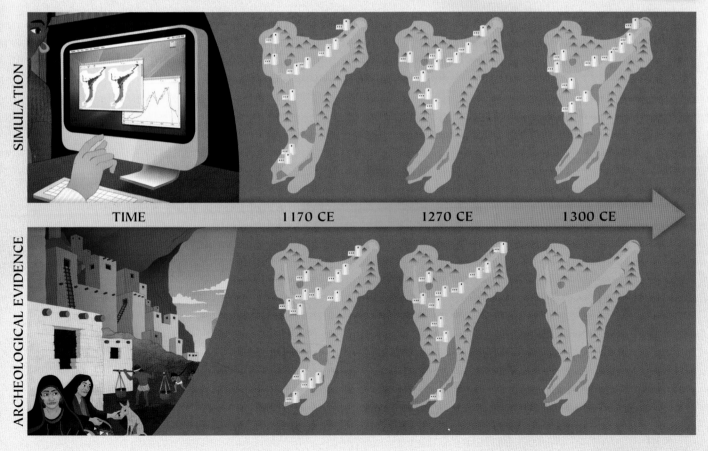

SIMULATION

ARCHEOLOGICAL EVIDENCE

TIME   1170 CE   1270 CE   1300 CE

MYSTERY SOLVED?

Scientists agree that the Anasazi people did not simply vanish. Rather, they migrated to other areas or merged with peoples whose descendants still live in the American Southwest.

But why? Thanks in part to the Artificial Anasazi Project, most scientists agree that environmental changes alone would not have caused all the Anasazi to evacuate the area. Other factors must have been at play. Researchers are studying the evidence and coming up with competing theories. Dean cautions, "Nearly every archaeologist has a personal opinion on how to interpret the archaeological and natural science data on the Anasazi abandonment of the Four Corners area in the late 1200s." There is still a lot of work to be done before this mystery is truly solved.

THE INVESTIGATION CONTINUES

... What combination of factors actually caused the Anasazi people to leave their homes?

The Anasazi did not have a written language and left no explanation of why they vanished. They did paint pictographs, such as this one on the rock surface at Anasazi Canyon, Utah; however so far their meaning is unknown to us.

Sir John Franklin

IT WAS 1984. OWEN BEATTIE, a forensic anthropologist from the University of Alberta, looked down from the small aircraft that was flying his crew into the Canadian Arctic. Beechey Island was below them. Shortly after the plane landed, Beattie stepped out into the chill air. Immediately, he saw three marked graves.

His team went to work. They unearthed John Torrington's grave first. As Beattie lifted the body of the young man to the surface of the permafrost, he said, "It's as if he's unconscious." But he wasn't. John Torrington had been dead for 138 years. The permafrost had turned his body into a natural mummy.

Beattie took bone, hair and tissue samples from the twenty-year-old's body. Torrington and his two companions were members of the fabled Franklin expedition. And Beattie, along with people the world over, wanted answers to some questions: Why had these three men died so early on in the expedition? And what had happened to Sir John Franklin and the rest of his crew?

Missing: Sir John Franklin — explorer

Date last seen: 1845

Place last seen: Melville Bay, Arctic

Possible reasons for disappearance:

lost, shipwrecked, starvation

BACKGROUND

In May 1845, Sir John Franklin set sail from England with two ships, the *Erebus* and the *Terror*. Franklin was a British Royal Navy officer and an experienced arctic explorer who had mapped almost two-thirds of North America's northern coastline. For this voyage, he had 134 men and enough supplies for a three-year trip. His mission? To find the elusive Northwest Passage.

Rumor had it that this channel between the Pacific and Atlantic Ocean could be found along the dangerous, iceberg-laden arctic coast of North America. No one knew if it truly existed.

At the time, trade ships moving between Europe and China had to journey around the southern tip of Africa. A Northwest Passage would allow Europeans a much shorter trip to Asia.

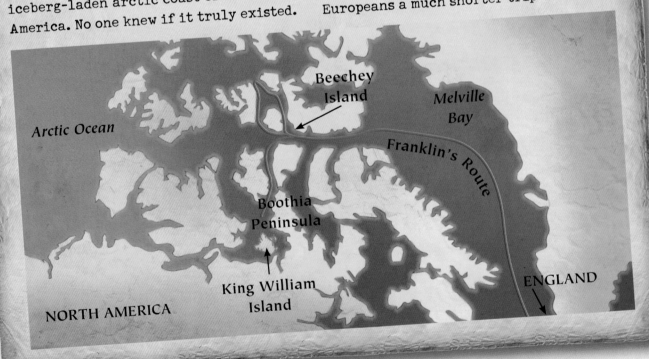

Arctic Ocean

Beechey Island

Melville Bay

Franklin's Route

Boothia Peninsula

King William Island

NORTH AMERICA

ENGLAND

The disappearance of Franklin and his ships prompted a landslide of search-and-rescue missions. Over thirty expeditions tried to find evidence of the missing men. In fact, more ships and men were lost looking for Franklin than were lost in Franklin's expedition itself!

For several years, search parties failed to find any clues. Then in 1850, shore parties from British and American search vessels discovered the graves of three of Franklin's crew members, a large empty stone cairn, or memorial, and signs of the men's first winter camp on tiny Beechey Island.

Four years later, trader and explorer John Rae was surveying the Boothia Peninsula when Inuit hunters showed him silver cutlery from Franklin's ships and even one of Franklin's medals. They had heard from others that Franklin's crew died from starvation, struggling to reach the shores of King William Island.

In May 1858, members of the Fox expedition, privately funded by John Franklin's widow, found signs of a hunting or observatory camp on King William Island. They discovered a skeleton and, under a rock cairn, two notes on a piece of paper in a cylinder, the only written record that has ever been found of Franklin's voyage.

What had become of Sir John Franklin and his crew? Would their bodies or their ships ever be found?

CASE OPEN

Historians now believe that Franklin's ships got trapped in the arctic ice in 1845 and that the crew spent their first winter on Beechey Island. The notes found by the Fox expedition reveal that during the winter of 1846–1847, Franklin's ships were trapped in the ice again, off the coast of King William Island. They did not break free of the ice the following spring. Franklin himself died in June 1847.

A full ten months later, the 105 remaining men filled their lifeboats with provisions, deserted the ships and headed across the ice toward King William Island. The second note also indicated a far-fetched notion: The men would try to march to Back's Fish River, a Hudson's Bay outpost that was 1900 km (1200 mi.) to the south.

South of the cairn, the Fox expedition found one of Franklin's ship's lifeboats on a

An excerpt from the note found by the Fox expedition: "The officers and crews consisting of 105 souls under the command of Captain F.R.M. Crozier landed here in Lat. 69° 37'42" Long. 98° 41' ... Sir John Franklin died on the 11th June 1847 and the total loss by deaths in the Expedition had been to this date 9 officers & 15 men."

sledge. Inside the boat were two skeletons and surprisingly frivolous items, such as button polish, slippers, hair combs and medals.

These discoveries sparked even more questions. Where was Franklin's grave? And what happened to the 105 remaining men the following spring? Another mystery: Why would the sailors have loaded the sledge with items that were of so little use?

The Lost Ships

Canadian Dave Woodman has searched for Franklin's lost ships for the past twenty-nine years. Knowing that Franklin's two ships had iron in their hulls and 14 tonne (15 ton) cast iron steam engines, Woodman has used magnetometers mounted in planes, ships, snowmobiles and sledges to look for signs of metal in his designated search area. He has investigated many magnetic anomalies or "targets," but all have turned out to be rocks. No ship remains have been found.

Enter Owen Beattie. The forensic anthropologist suspected that some answers lay within the bodies of Franklin's crew members. In 1986, he made his visit to Beechey Island to get bone, hair and tissue samples from John Torrington, John Hartnell and William Braine, the first three victims of Franklin's expedition.

Back home, Beattie's colleagues analyzed the bone and hair samples using atomic absorption spectroscopy. They dissolved the samples of John Torrington's hair in nitric acid and then heated them to extremely high temperatures. The samples turned to vapor and were then passed through a spectrometer. A spectrometer can reveal the atomic makeup of a sample. Scientists saw that John Torrington's results showed high amounts of a foreign material: lead. In fact, Torrington's hair tissues contained 120 times the amount of lead typically found in hair. Tests on the other two bodies gave similar results.

But where had the lead come from? On one of his earlier voyages, Franklin and his crew had almost starved to death. This time, his expedition had been supplied with enough food for three years: 8000 tins of provisions — all soldered, or sealed, with a mixture of lead and tin. Beattie took ten samples of the tin cans and tested the levels of lead in them. Lab tests proved the lead levels were extremely high.

Beattie explains, "We found that the lead used to seal the cans of food was the same isotope signature as the lead in the sailors' tissues. As no other logical lead-containing items on the expedition had the same signatures, we are very certain that the canned foods were the culprits."

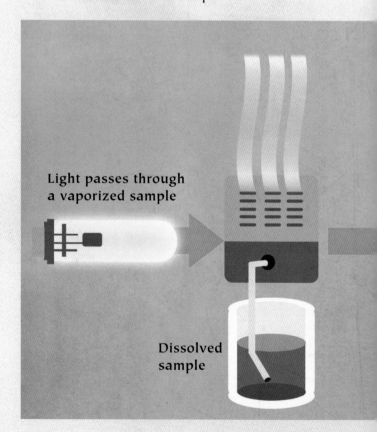

Light passes through a vaporized sample

Dissolved sample

Lead Evidence

Beattie knew the sailors had not been poisoned back home. When lead is breathed into the body, or ingested in food or water, it stays for a relatively short time in soft tissues like hair. Finding lead in the sailor's hair meant that Torrington had been exposed to lead soon before he died. Most certainly, the lead was from the expedition food.

The cans Beattie tested had not been properly soldered. Beads of solder were applied to the interior edges of the cans. This allowed the lead to leach into the food.

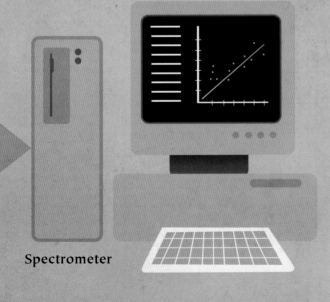

The spectrometer analyzes the amount of light that passes through the sample and reveals its atomic makeup.

Spectrometer

Beattie explains, "In our investigation of the Franklin expedition disaster, we used both new and old 'technology.' That is, part of our research was to investigate the physical remains of some of the crew members ... So, we could identify features such as healed broken bones or signs of diseases (like tuberculosis), and these observations were made using medical knowledge already established by the mid-1800s. However, this information was made more important through the application of new medical and scientific knowledge and techniques, such as X-ray imaging, trace element analysis and so on."

MYSTERY SOLVED?

Such high amounts of lead would have contaminated the food and poisoned the men. The effects would have ranged from loss of appetite to loss of muscle control. Lead poisoning can damage internal organs and weaken bodies, putting them at higher risk of catching other diseases, such as tuberculosis, scurvy and pneumonia. It can even seriously affect brain functioning.

For example, Beattie speculates that lead poisoning may have caused Franklin's crew to pack a sledge with useless items that they then struggled to haul across the ice. "If crew members were suffering from lead poisoning, they might have irrational behaviors, possibly leading to dangerous decisions in an unforgiving arctic environment. In total, it could have been a devastating problem on this expedition."

Clues about the tragedy of the Franklin expedition continue to trickle in. Several sites on King William Island containing bones and skulls also show signs of lead poisoning. But neither the *Terror* nor the *Erebus* has ever been located, nor the body of John Franklin himself.

These are the graves on Beechey Island of the three members of the Franklin Expedition who died in the winter of 1846. The men were buried when the ground thawed in the spring. Torrington's gravestone reads "Sacred to the memory of John Torrington, who departed this life January 1st, A.D. 1846, on board of HM ship Terror, aged 20 years" Up the hill is a fourth grave, that of a sailor who came searching for the Expedition in 1854.

THE INVESTIGATION CONTINUES

... The main questions remain: Where is Franklin's grave? Where are his ships, the *Terror* and *Erebus*?

Anastasia

IT WAS JULY 2007. A group of amateur history buffs was spending yet another summer week-end investigating the woods near Yekaterinburg in southern Russia. The site had been searched before, fruitlessly. Nevertheless, the group was convinced that previous searches had not covered the whole area.

One of the men, Sergei Plotnikov, was probing the ground in a hollow surrounded by silver birch trees, close to the main road. Suddenly, he heard a crunch. He knew it meant he had either hit charcoal … or bone.

Plotnikov began to dig with a friend. And then they saw them — bone fragments from a pelvis and then a skull. Had they done it? Had they actually found the skeletons of Anastasia, the lost princess of Russia, and her brother, Alexei?

Missing: Anastasia — Russian princess

Date last seen: July 1918

Place last seen: Yekaterinburg, Russia

Possible reasons for disappearance: murdered and buried in unknown grave, escaped

BACKGROUND

Princess Anastasia and Prince Alexei were the youngest children of Nicholas Romanov II, the last czar of Russia. The House of Romanov had ruled Russia for about 300 years. But more and more of the Russian people wanted to end the rule of monarchy. In 1905, they revolted, starting a chain of turmoil that led to the February Revolution of 1917. Nicholas was forced to give up his throne. A temporary government was formed in the capital city of Petrograd. The Romanovs, parents and children, were put under house arrest.

In August 1917, the Romanovs were moved to Siberia, supposedly to protect them from the royalist-hating Bolshevik party. Then in the October Revolution of 1917, the Bolsheviks seized power. The following spring, they exiled the royal family to their home in Yekaterinburg.

Fearing for their lives, the Romanovs still hoped for rescue from their loyal followers. But the Bolsheviks made a drastic decision. On the night of July 16, the Romanovs were awakened from their sleep. They were taken into the cellar with their three servants and physician, and lined up in front of a firing squad of secret police. An officer gave the order to fire.

At the time, it was uncertain exactly what had happened next. Headlines in the paper told of the czar's death, but no one knew the location of his grave. Rumors circulated that not all the children had been killed, that at least one of the Romanov children — maybe Princess Anastasia and even Prince Alexei — had somehow survived the massacre. Stories told of sympathetic guards rescuing Anastasia. People claimed to have seen her afterwards, wounded but alive. The tales and speculation were fueled for decades by the Communist (formerly Bolshevik) government's secrecy and cover up.

Had the two royal children escaped and survived? And where were the bodies of the Romanov family?

CASE OPEN

Alexander Avdonin, an amateur historian, was driven to find out what had happened to the Romanovs. In 1979, filmmaker and former police officer Geli Ryabov helped him gain access to secret documents. Avdonin scoured them for clues. One source mentioned that the executioners had been planning to dump the bodies in a local mine shaft, but their truck broke down. Instead, the executioners burned the bodies with gasoline and then poured acid on the bones to make them unrecognizable. Then they threw the bones in a shallow pit near the road and covered them with dirt.

From these details and other historical materials, Avdonin and Ryabov figured out the general location of the grave. They did some digging and, incredibly, turned up several skulls and bones! However, the men were nervous about how the government might respond to their discovery. They only photographed the bones and made casts of the skulls. The next summer, they returned the bones to their burial site — and kept quiet.

In the late 1980s, the Soviet Union collapsed, ending Communist rule. The smoldering questions about the lost Romanovs flamed again. Government files were opened to the public, and in 1989, Ryabov announced that he had found the royal family's remains.

In the summer of 1991, Avdonin led a search team to the remains. The skeletons of nine bodies were exhumed. The following year, Peter Gill of the Forensic Science Service in Berkshire, England, and forensic scientist Pavel L. Ivanov, of the Russian Academy of Sciences, were asked to conduct DNA tests on the remains.

Spotlight on DNA

DNA is found in almost all human cells. Long pieces of DNA, called chromosomes, carry the instructions for making life. Your DNA, for example, contains the "recipe" for making the proteins that determine your physical traits, such as your eye color, racial features and risk of getting certain diseases.

Information in the DNA is passed down from one generation to the next in the cell nucleus.

DNA is also found in another part of the cell, the mitochondrion. This small structure creates energy for the cell to use. Mitochondrial DNA (mtDNA) comes from eggs, so nearly all of it is inherited from the mother. This means that your mtDNA is exactly the same as your mother's, which makes mtDNA a powerful tool for tracking ancestry and confirming people's identities.

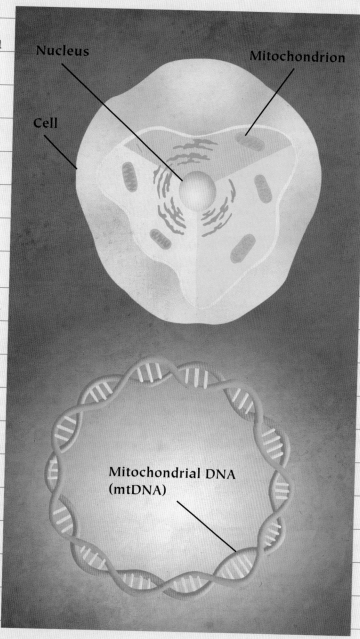

Nucleus

Mitochondrion

Cell

Mitochondrial DNA
(mtDNA)

The Romanov children from left to right: Maria, Tatiana, Anastasia, Olga, Alexei

Gill and Ivanov extracted DNA from the bones in the pit. First, they determined the genders in the samples by looking at two chromosomes, the X chromosome and the Y chromosome. Females have two X chromosomes, and males have one X and one Y. The scientists established that five females and four males were among the remains. But were any of them Romanovs?

The scientists next compared the mitochondrial DNA of the nine bodies. The mtDNA of one adult and three children matched samples from one of Czarina Alexandra's maternal relatives. The mtDNA of the other adult body matched samples from two of Czar Nicholas's maternal relatives. So the scientists were almost certain that these five bodies were all members of the Romanov family.

However, there were still two children's bodies missing — Alexei, aged 13, and a daughter, either Maria, 19, or Anastasia, 17.

Saved by the Jewels?

Historical records showed that the Romanov girls had sewn their jewels and gemstones into the linings of their corsets in the hope that their riches might one day help them. Some historians explain that this may be why the bullets fired on the girls had difficulty piercing their bodies. Might the jewels have actually deflected the bullets, saving the life of at least one princess?

[Top] Anastasia Romanov, [Bottom] Anna Anderson

Over the years, many women had come forward, claiming to be the youngest Romanov daughter. The most famous was "Anna Anderson," who was rescued after she jumped into a canal in Germany in 1922. Many people, including handwriting experts and members of the Romanov family, believed her claims. But skeptics thought she was actually a Polish factory worker, Franciszka Szanckowska, who had disappeared shortly before Anderson appeared. Could Anna Anderson's claims of being Anastasia have been true? Perhaps DNA testing could answer this question.

Anderson passed away in 1984, but tissues from her body had been kept. Peter Gill compared samples of Anderson's DNA with

that of the Romanovs and of Prince Philip of England (who is a royal relative). Gill's team also found a maternal grandnephew of Franciszka Szanckowska in Germany, named Karl Maucher, who agreed to have his DNA analyzed. If Anderson's DNA samples matched Prince Philip's, they would know Anderson was related to the Romanovs. If the samples matched Maucher's, this would mean she was related to him — and was not a Romanov.

The DNA tests showed that Anna Anderson was actually Franciszka Szanckowska of Poland.

Anna Anderson	C T G T T C T T T C A T G G G G A A G C A G A T T	
Carl Maucher	C T G T T C T T T C A T G G G G A A G C A G A T T	25
Prince Philip	C T G T T C T T T C A T G G G G A A G C A G A T T	
Anna Anderson	T G G G T A C C A C C C A A G T A T T G A C T C A	
Carl Maucher	T G G G T A C C A C C C A A G T A T T G A C T C A	50
Prince Philip	T G G G T A C C A C C C A A G T A T T G A C T C A	
Anna Anderson	C C C A T C A A C A A C C G C T A T G T A T T T C	
Carl Maucher	C C C A T C A A C A A C C G C T A T G T A T T T C	75
Prince Philip	C C C A T C A A C A A C C G C T A T G T A T T T C	
Anna Anderson	G T A C A T T A C T G C C A G C C A C C A T G A A	
Carl Maucher	G T A C A T T A C T G C C A G C C A C C A T G A A	100
Prince Philip	G T A C A T T A C T G C C A G T C A C C A T G A A	
Anna Anderson	T A T T G C A C G G T A C C A T A A A T A C T T G	
Carl Maucher	T A T T G C A C G G T A C C A T A A A T A C T T G	125
Prince Philip	T A T T G T A C G G T A C C A T A A A T A C T T G	
Anna Anderson	A C C A C C T G T A G T A C A T A A A A A C C C A	
Carl Maucher	A C C A C C T G T A G T A C A T A A A A A C C C A	150
Prince Philip	A C C A C C T G T A G T A C A T A A A A A C C C A	
Anna Anderson	A T C C A C A T C A A A A C C C C C T C C C C A T	
Carl Maucher	A T C C A C A T C A A A A C C C C C T C C C C A T	175
Prince Philip	A T C C A C A T C A A A A C C C C C T C C C C A T	
Anna Anderson	G C T T A C A A G C A A G T A C A G C A A T C A A	
Carl Maucher	G C T T A C A A G C A A G T A C A G C A A T C A A	200
Prince Philip	G C T T A C A A G C A A G T A C A G C A A T C A A	
Anna Anderson	C C C T C A A C T A T C A C A C A T C A A C T G C	
Carl Maucher	C C C T C A A C T A T C A C A C A T C A A C T G C	225
Prince Philip	C C C T C A A C T A T C A C A C A T C A A C T G C	
Anna Anderson	A A C T C C A A A G C C A C C C C T C A T C C A C	
Carl Maucher	A A C T C C A A A G C C A C C C C T C A T C C A C	250
Prince Philip	A A C T C C A A A G C C A C C C C T C A C C C A C	
Anna Anderson	T A G G A T A C C A A C A A A C C T A C C C A C C	
Carl Maucher	T A G G A T A C C A A C A A A C C T A C C C A C C	275
Prince Philip	T A G G A T A C C A A C A A A C C T A C C C A C C	
Anna Anderson	C T T A A C A G C A C A T A G T A C A T A A A G C	
Carl Maucher	C T T A A C A G C A C A T A G T A C A T A A A G C	300
Prince Philip	C T T A A C A G T A C A T A G T A C A T A A A G C	
Anna Anderson	C A T T T A C C G T A C A T A G C A C A T T A T A	
Carl Maucher	C A T T T A C C G T A C A T A G C A C A T T A T A	325
Prince Philip	C A T T T A C C G T A C A T A G C A C A T T A C A	
Anna Anderson	G T C A A A T C C C T T C T C G T C C C C A T G G	
Carl Maucher	G T C A A A T C C C T T C T C G T C C C C A T G G	350
Prince Philip	G T C A A A T C C C T C C T C G T C C C C A T G G	
Anna Anderson	A T G A C C C C C C T C A G A T A G G G G T C C C	
Carl Maucher	A T G A C C C C C C T C A G A T A G G G G T C C C	375
Prince Philip	A T G A C C C C C C T C A G A T A G G G G T C C C	
Anna Anderson	T T G A C	
Carl Maucher	T T G A C	400
Prince Philip	T T G A C	

The results of a test comparing the DNA of Anna Anderson, Karl Maucher and Prince Philip.

Another Royal Claim

A tombstone in Burnaby, British Columbia, reads, "Romanov, His Imperial Highness, Alexei Nicolaievich, Sovereign Heir, Tsarevich, Grand Duke of Russia, August 12, 1904, June 26, 1977." The man buried there, Heino Tammet, asserted he was the youngest son of the Czar. Was this man truly Alexei? A new DNA discovery may effectively disprove his claim.

So then how to explain the two missing bodies? This remained a burning question for many Russians and royalists the world over, including the members of an historical club based in Yekaterinburg. Determined to find the disappeared Romanovs, they studied historical reports about the executions. They noticed that a Bolshevik soldier had mentioned burying two of the bodies apart from the others. He said that another grave was "nearby."

The club members returned to the place where the Romanov remains had been found in 1979. They spent several summer weekends in 2007 exploring the wooded site near Yekaterinburg. And then, in late July, came Sergei Plotnikov's incredible discovery of the bones. Using metal detectors and metal rods as probes, club members and archaeologists also discovered shards of a ceramic container, nails, metal strips from a wooden box and bullets of various calibers.

DNA tests confirmed the bodies were the remains of siblings Prince Alexei and, likely, Princess Maria — not Anastasia.

The Lost Princes in the Tower

DNA testing could solve another royal mystery. When King Edward IV of England died in 1483, his eldest son, thirteen-year-old Edward, was crowned. But six weeks later, the boy's uncle, Richard, declared himself king. He confined Edward and his ten-year-old brother, Richard, to the Tower of London. After July that year, the princes were never seen again.

In 1674, demolition workers at the Tower discovered two skeletons at the bottom of a staircase. King Charles II ordered that "the supposed bodyes of ye two Princes" be placed in an urn and stored at Westminster Abbey.

Were the bodies, in fact, those of the lost princes? British medieval historian John Ashdown-Hill wants to find out for certain. He suggests comparing mtDNA from the bones in the urn with that of Mary Tudor, the princes' niece. Samples of Mary's hair were taken and preserved in lockets when her tomb was opened in the 1800s. Ashdown-Hill has been given permission to try to extract DNA from these hair samples. There may be one obstacle, however. In the past, authorities have not allowed the bones in the urn to be unearthed. Without the bones, it will be impossible to compare Mary Tudor's DNA samples with those of the skeletons.

MYSTERY SOLVED?

Despite all the rumors, all the pretenders to her name, Anastasia had never been missing after all. In fact, there was finally scientific proof that, sadly, none of the Romanov children had survived the massacre. "We now have close to definite proof that the entire family was executed by the Bolsheviks, and no one escaped," reported Gill in 2008. "There is overwhelming evidence that the remains found in the second grave are those of Alexei and one of the Romanov princesses."

DNA evidence could only prove that the two remains were Romanov siblings. It couldn't prove which ones. But scientists studied the bones and, from these, determined the age of each set of remains. Most scientists concluded that one sibling was Alexei and the other was Anastasia's older sister, Maria.

Anastasia (left) and Maria share a quiet moment. (This photo was taken sometime between 1908 and 1915.)

On July 17, 1998, the remains of Czar Nicholas and Czarina Alexandra, and their children Anastasia, Olga and Tatiana were buried in St. Peter and Paul Cathedral, in St. Petersburg, Russia, the traditional burial site of the Romanov czars. In 2008 — ninety years after the execution of the royal family — the remains of Alexei and Maria were finally reunited with those of their family members.

THE INVESTIGATION CONTINUES

... What other mysteries of lost identity will DNA testing solve?

George L. Mallory

ON MAY 1, 1999, JOCHEN HEMMLEB stood at a base camp on Mount Everest, radio in hand. Above, out of sight, a five-man climbing team headed across the North Face of Mount Everest. It was Hemmleb who had carefully outlined their search route. He listened in as the climbers fanned westward across the area known as the Snow Terrace, traveling toward the "rib" in the distance.

After half an hour, the radio crackled to life with a cryptic message including a secret code. Hemmleb recalls, "The suspense was almost unbearable — but I knew deep inside that they had made the big find." Hemmleb was referring to the missing bodies of the world-famous mountain climber George Leigh Mallory and his climbing partner Andrew Irvine, who had disappeared seventy-five years ago. Had the team found one of the men, and if so, which one?

Missing: George Leigh Mallory — mountain climber

Date last seen: June 8, 1924

Place last seen: Mount Everest

Possible reasons for disappearance: fell to death, altitude sickness, froze to death

BACKGROUND

In 1924, British climber George Leigh Mallory and a young member of his expedition, Andrew Irvine, attempted to climb Mount Everest, the highest mountain in the world. At the time, there were two main routes up the mountain, one on the south side and one on the north side. On the morning of June 6, Mallory and Irvine headed up the mountain's North Ridge route. They hoped to reach the summit in three days.

Noel Odell was following behind the two men as support. On the afternoon of June 8, Odell saw the two climbers, Mallory and Irvine, moving up the mountain's skyline. They had just reached the major rock "step" called the Second Step, 275 m (900 ft.) from the summit, when clouds formed, and the men vanished from his sight. Mallory and Irvine would never be seen alive again.

In the 1930s, mountain climbers on the North Ridge route found the remains of Mallory's last and highest camp, including a working flashlight and unused emergency flares. In 1933, a team came across an ice axe on Everest's Northeast Ridge at about 8450 m (27 730 ft.). It had three nicks on the wooden handle, a mark Irvine occasionally used to identify his belongings.

The Chinese government closed the Tibetan border in 1950. This meant access to the North Ridge route was closed to foreigners. In 1975, a Chinese team climbing Mount Everest set up camp at 8170 m (26 800 ft.). Four years later, Chinese climber Wang Hong Bao described how he found the body of a Caucasian, an "English dead," about a ten minute walk from the campsite. Wang could tell the climber's body had been there for many years. When he touched the climber's clothes, the fabric fell apart.

Had Wang found Andrew Irvine? Had Irvine fallen from the place where his ice axe was discovered? Tragically, Wang Hong Bao died the day after his revelation, without sharing further details about the exact location of the body or his camp. The mysteries remained: Where were the bodies of Mallory and Irvine? And had the men made it to the top of Everest before vanishing?

CASE OPEN

Jochen Hemmleb, a German mountain historian, first learned of the disappearance of Mallory and Irvine when he was six years old. He had been haunted by it ever since. He co-initiated the Mallory & Irvine Research Expedition, and his role was critical: to figure out the most likely location of the missing bodies. Hemmleb believed that the sighting of the "English dead" was key evidence. He decided to work backward from that point: "By locating the site of the 1975 Chinese Camp VI … we could put ourselves in the footsteps of that Chinese climber — going where he went, and hopefully again finding the 'English dead.'"

Going Up!

Climbing Everest takes days. Teams camp overnight as they work their way up. Camps are often numbered in order. The higher the camp, the higher the number.

Hemmleb knew that Chinese Camp VI was set up at 8170 m (26 800 ft.), but where exactly on Everest? Was it on Everest's North Ridge itself or lower down, on the face of the mountain? Only one photo from the Chinese expedition showed some background features, which included a triangular snowfield.

Hemmleb took a closer look at other photographs taken in the area and realized that ones taken from the upper North Ridge and facing the summit all had one thing in common: the triangular snowfield. Hemmleb compared the photo with an orthophotograph of Everest.

(An orthophotograph is a special bird's-eye-view photo that shows distances as accurately as a map.) He marked distinct features on both images and then connected the dots. The spot where they met was the place where the photograph was taken — Chinese Camp VI!

Jochen Hemmleb calculated that the camp was on the North Face, but farther out on the North Face than other Chinese campsites had ever been. It was on a rib of rock, far from any modern climber's path to the summit. "No wonder nobody had found the Chinese camp after 1975!" says Hemmleb.

Photographs taken from the air are often distorted for several reasons, such as the tilt of the camera and the curve of the Earth. For example, if you take an aerial photo of two snowfields that are of equal size but are at different altitudes on a mountain, the one closer to the camera will appear larger. Distortions like these are removed in orthophotographs such as the one above.

In the spring of 1999, armed with Hemmleb's calculations, the Mallory & Irvine Research Expedition headed to Mount Everest. They brought a metal detector to search for snow-covered artifacts (such as Mallory's camera) and signs of the men's bodies (such as the nails in their boots). The team planned to mark the site of the ice axe, and other artifacts, with a GPS. They would document the search with video and still cameras.

The expedition set up a Camp V site. From there, on the morning of May 1, the search team — made up of Tap Richards, Conrad Anker, Dave Hahn, Andy Politz and Jake Norton — climbed to the 8170 m (26 800 ft.) height. Hemmleb had marked out four search routes. He explains, "By knowing the location of the Chinese camp, we had a considerably smaller area to search."

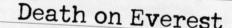

(below) Photo taken at Chinese Camp VI

Hemmleb waited at base camp, far below, as the climbers began their investigation. They had difficulty moving along the steeply sloping mountain face at such a high altitude. Every step had to be carefully placed. They fanned out, climbing up, down and across the face of the mountain, looking at the terrain and trying to figure out what might have gone so terribly wrong there seventy-five years ago.

Soon, Anker discovered a body. But its modern clothing revealed that it was a mountain climber who had died more recently. The climbers found another body, and then another one, mangled and frozen. They realized they were in a sort of catchment basin, which was "gathering" fallen mountaineers. Each time team members located a body, they radioed Hemmleb to describe their find. From the clothing and equipment, however, they knew none of the bodies were Andrew Irvine or George Leigh Mallory.

First Step

Third Step

Snow gutter

Triangular snowfield

Death on Everest

Climbing Everest is dangerous. Climbers face the possibility of frostbite, altitude sickness, hypothermia and snow blindness. Only about one in four people are successful. Even now, with the best training and technology, people still die on Everest. There are about 120 bodies frozen on the mountain. It is too difficult and dangerous to remove them all.

Conrad Anker had climbed farthest down the mountain. At 11:45 A.M., he began climbing back toward his teammates when he saw another frozen body, almost perfectly preserved. On his head was a leather cap; on his foot was a hobnail boot. He had been wrapped in seven or eight layers of clothing, but most of it had been torn away by wind, revealing skin bleached white. The man's right elbow was dislocated or broken; his right leg was broken. A rope was tied to his waist, broken at one end. Clearly, the man had been tied to a partner at one time … Was this Irvine?

Anker alerted the other climbers over the radio with their secret code. The team gathered around the body. They knew from the old-fashioned climbing clothes that the corpse was decades old. They also knew that no one except Mallory and Irvine had died on Everest at this altitude between 1924 and 1938. They assumed they had discovered Andrew Irvine. But when the men examined the body closely, they found name tags sewn into the clothing: G. Mallory. This was the body Wang had seen, but it was Mallory, not Irvine!

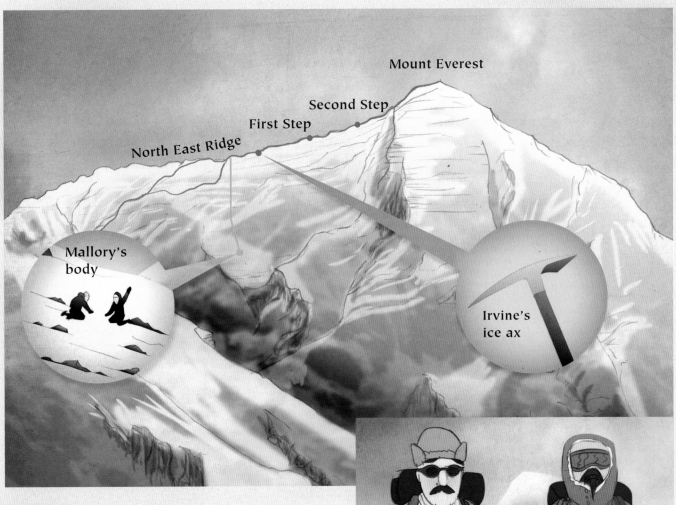

Mount Everest

Second Step

First Step

North East Ridge

▲ Mallory's body

Irvine's ice ax

The climbers took many photographs of the body and the site. Then they spent hours chipping away at the ice, looking for artifacts in Mallory's clothing. They found several items, including a pencil, a pair of goggles, a pair of nail scissors and several letters wrapped in a monogrammed handkerchief. Unable to move the body frozen into place on the mountainside, the men covered it with stones, and then Politz read aloud a funeral service.

In the meantime, Hemmleb was watching the events through binoculars from base camp, but could only tell that the men were examining a body. He received no more radio transmissions; the team did not want to alert other climbers who might have been using the same radio frequency. But before the end of the day, Anker sent Hemmleb a simple message: "Jochen, you are going to be a happy man."

The climber on the left wears clothing similar to what Mallory and Irvine would have worn: up to seven layers of wool, silk and cotton clothing, with an outer layer of gabardine, all fastened with buttons. The climber on the right wears modern synthetic clothing, including polypropylene underclothes, complete with zippers.

MYSTERY SOLVED?

Mallory's body was found, but the hunt for Irvine's body continues. Expeditions also continue to search for the one, or perhaps two, cameras that historians believe Mallory and Irvine took on their climb up Everest. Photos could solve the riddle of whether or not the men ever reached the summit.

In 2007, a team of climbers from the Altitude Everest Expedition tried to answer this question by recreating Mallory and Irvine's climb. One of the climbers was Conrad Anker,

Mallory & Irvine Research Expedition, 1999 (standing from left to right): Lee Meyers, Conrad Anker, Andy Politz, Dave Hahn, Thom Pollard, Jake Norton, Tap Richards, Eric Simonson and (sitting) Jochen Hemmleb

the man who had discovered Mallory's body in 1999. For some parts of the climb, team members wore clothing similar to what Mallory and Irvine would have worn, for example, wool and silk clothing and leather equipment.

After reaching the summit and then descending, Anker reported that he believed it possible that Mallory and Irvine had reached the summit — but not likely.

CASE CLOSED

... But where is the body of Andrew Irvine?

Star Dust

IN JANUARY 1998, TWO YOUNG mountain climbers from Buenos Aires were standing near the edge of the glacier on Mount Tupungato when they noticed a small engine sitting on a hunk of ice. On its side were the words " – OLLS ROYCE."

The mountain, part of the Andes mountain range, is one of the highest peaks in South America. So what was an engine doing at this altitude in the middle of nowhere? Puzzled, the climbers scanned the area. They found sections of airplane wings and parts of an airplane body, as well as some electrical wiring. They also came across fragments of clothing. Oddly, the material was patterned in a way that had not been in fashion for … well, for decades. The pair noted their findings without recording their location and then headed off, refocused on their climb.

A civilian search team relocated the wreckage two years later and found human remains. Now the Argentinean military became involved. The air force asked Dr. Carlos Bauzá to help investigate the site. The Argentinean medical doctor was a climber and airplane pilot. He had helped investigate two previous aircraft accidents, and he'd heard the rumors about this one. Could it be true? Did the wreckage really belong to the *Star Dust*?

Missing: *Star Dust* — airplane

Date last seen: August 2, 1947

Place last seen: Buenos Aires, Argentina

Possible reasons for disappearance: bomb,

    mechanical malfunction

BACKGROUND

On August 2, 1947, an airliner named *Star Dust* took off from a scheduled stopover in Buenos Aires, Argentina. The commercial flight was on its way to Santiago, Chile, from London, England. It carried eleven passengers. At 5:33 P.M., the air traffic control tower at Santiago received a message from *Star Dust*'s radio operator: The plane was slightly behind schedule but would arrive in about twelve minutes.

Star Dust sent its final transmission

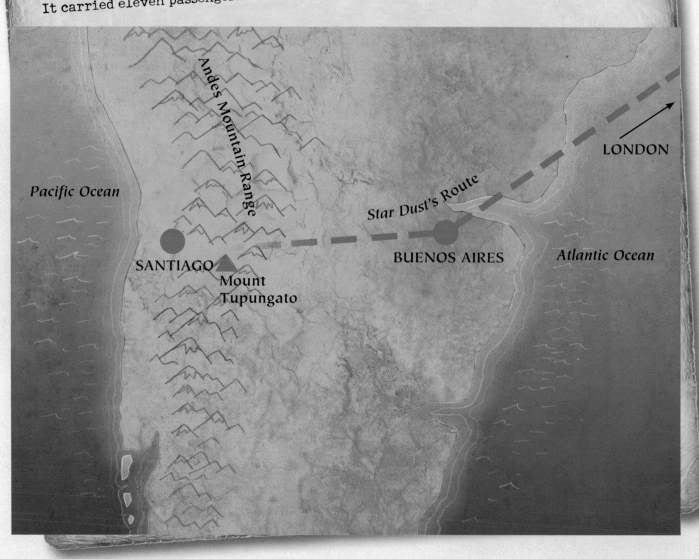

in Morse code when the airplane was four minutes away from arrival: S-T-E-N-D-E-C. The Chilean Morse code operator radioed back, asking for clarification. The message was sent two more times, and then *Star Dust* fell silent. It was never heard from again. Nor did it ever arrive at its destination. In fact, the plane completely vanished.

Aviation experts calculated that the plane must have slammed into Mount Tupungato. A search team was sent out, but no trace of the airplane was found. Some thought that it had been blown up.

Some believed it may have overshot land and gone down into the Pacific Ocean. Others even wondered if the plane had been abducted by aliens. For decades, mountaineers visited the slopes of Mount Tupungato, but none of them ever spotted any wreckage.

So how could it be that over fifty years later, an engine could appear on the mountainside? Why had the plane crashed? Where had the wreckage been all those years? And what was the meaning of *Star Dust*'s final transmission?

CASE OPEN

On February 17, 2000, Dr. Bauzá led an investigative team of 100 Argentinean soldiers into the Andes. For days, they traveled uphill by truck. After establishing a base camp, they continued up the steep mountain trails by mule. On February 21, twelve team members climbed on foot in the extreme cold. When they reached the Tupungato glacier at 4700 m (15 400 ft.), they set up tents.

The next morning, the team began searching for the plane wreck amid a snowstorm. Bauzá recalls, "By noon, we saw the first remainders of the *Star Dust*." Using a GPS, they carefully recorded the location of every piece of plane they found. Later, they would analyze the wreckage to try to learn what caused the crash.

The team found the two main wheels of the plane, still in their normal flying position. Bauzá notes, "One of the wheels was completely inflated. This showed me that at the moment of the collision against the mountain, the wheels had not been lowered. This was a new insight, to think that *Star Dust* was not in an emergency situation."

The Rolls-Royce engine of Star Dust, photographed in 2000

Bauzá also found the propeller, scarred and bent back. From this he could tell that the propeller was still spinning when the plane crashed. The discovery was significant. In an emergency, the pilot would have swiveled the blades of the propeller to offer less resistance. Bauzá explains, "As the blades were not in this streamlined position, this indicates that the motor was functioning normally at the moment of the impact." In other words, engine failure did not cause the plane to go down.

Sabotage was also ruled out. If the plane had been blown up in midair, the debris would have been scattered far and wide. Instead, the debris was crushed and in a contained area. It began to look like the plane had flown straight into the glacier at high speed. However, Bauzá was puzzled: "If the fuselage had experienced a frontal impact, the pressure would have come from a single direction. But the parts of the fuselage that we recovered were deformed in ways that told us there had been pressure on it from different angles."

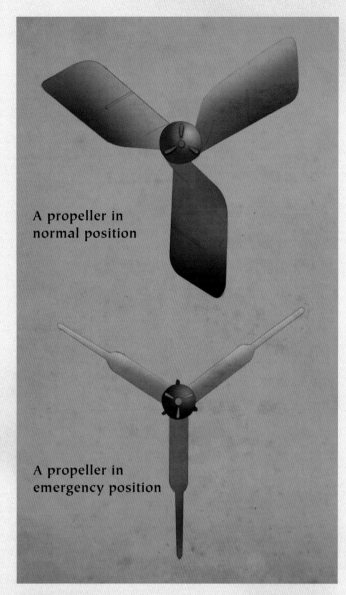

A propeller in normal position

A propeller in emergency position

Imagine taking an aluminum can by its base and slamming it against a wall. Now picture taking an aluminum can and crumpling it from all directions with your hands. The differences between the two cans would be obvious. And each can would show evidence of how it had been damaged. The same is true of an airplane. The plane that had crashed head-on would look different than a plane that was hit from the side, blown apart from within or damaged from all sides.

Bauzá and an air crash investigator colleague, Carlos Sorini, began working with a new theory: What if the plane had not fallen directly where they found the wreckage? They presented the evidence to Juan Carlos Leiva, a glaciologist (an expert on glaciers). Leiva concluded that the plane likely crashed higher up the mountain, causing vibrations, which triggered an avalanche that buried the remains of the plane. Over time, the wreckage became part of the glacier, traveling downhill deep inside of it. The moving ice and stones ground against the plane parts, putting pressure on them from many angles and causing increased damage. When the wreckage reached the lower part of the mountain, warmer temperatures melted the surface of the glacier, revealing the plane parts beneath.

But one question remained: Why did *Star Dust* crash into the mountainside?

Star Dust, a Lancastrian airliner, was one of the few planes at the time that could fly above 7300 m (24 000 ft.). Bauzá believes that the crew saw bad weather ahead and decided to steer above the mountains to avoid it. Analysis of old weather charts shows that this meant the pilots flew the plane straight into a jet stream. But the crew wouldn't have been aware of it. At the time, not much was known about this meteorological phenomenon.

Investigators believe the winds in the jet stream could have been blowing against *Star Dust* at about 160 km/h (100 m.p.h.). This would have slowed the plane considerably, without the crew realizing it. At the time, pilots navigated with knowledge of wind conditions on the ground and sightings taken from the airplane windows. The conditions over the Andes had been cloudy. The crew likely thought they had crossed to the other side of the mountain range — but they hadn't. When they began to descend, they were aimed straight for the mountainside. *Star Dust* would have hit the mountain and, seconds after the crash, vanished under an avalanche.

Jet streams are high-speed winds that circle the globe at about 6 to 10 km (4 to 6 mi.) above Earth's surface. (They are also known to exist on Jupiter!) These bands of winds form where warm and cold air meet. Their average speeds are between 80 and 160 km/h (50 and 100 m.p.h.), but they can reach up to 400 km/h (250 m.p.h.). Commercial aircraft often try to travel with a jet stream to dramatically boost speed and reduce fuel consumption.

Star Dust likely caused an avalanche on impact.

Over time the wreckage traveled downhill inside a glacier.

Warmer temperatures revealed parts of the plane.

The Search for Amelia Earhart

Lack of scientific technology meant all early airplane flights faced more risk than flights do today. On June 1, 1937, ten years before the disappearance of *Star Dust*, record-breaking aviator Amelia Earhart and her navigator, Fred Noonan, set off to be first to fly around the world. On July 2, one month into the trip, they took off in their twin-engine Lockheed Electra. They were flying from Lae, New Guinea, and headed for their next stop, tiny Howland Island, 4113 km (2556 mi.)

distant, in the middle of the vast Pacific Ocean. At 8:45 the next morning, the United States Coast Guard heard Earhart's last transmission. Then her airplane vanished.

The United States launched the largest air and sea search in naval history but found nothing. Mysteries abound. In 1940, a navigational tool called a sextant and a human skeleton were found on an uninhabited island (today's Nikumaroro). More recently, other artifacts have been found on the island, including an aluminum panel, a piece of clear Plexiglas (the thickness and curvature of an Electra window) and a women's size 9 heel dating from the 1930s. There are those who believe that, like *Star Dust*, Earhart's plane was swept away by natural forces. Perhaps it was carried off the island reef by ocean tides to where it now lies waiting to be recovered.

MYSTERY SOLVED?

Star Dust has certainly been found. And it seems clear that the aircraft flew into the side of Mount Tupungato. The debris itself is the evidence. "This type of accident is called CFIT (Controlled Flight Into Terrain)," says Bauzá.

The science behind the jet stream analysis is also convincing. And time will certainly tell if the glacier theory is correct. Bauzá expects up to 90% of the wreckage to show up at the edge of the glacier on Mount Tupungato.

The Andes mountain range, beautiful but treacherous, is the final resting place of Star Dust and its eleven passengers. Carlos Bauzá recalls standing on the slopes of Mount Tupungato: "When I was in the place where we found the remains, I realized that the plane could not have fallen directly there, a hole among the high mountains."

CASE CLOSED

... But what is the meaning of *Star Dust*'s final transmission, S-T-E-N-D-E-C?

INS Dakar

"DONNA!" CALLED OUT the sonar equipment operator. "Can you have a look?"

Donna Johnson headed over to the computer screen. She was the expert sonar imaging analyst on the ship *Flying Enterprise*. Their team had been towing sonar equipment in the Mediterranean Sea twenty-four hours a day, looking for a submarine that had vanished almost thirty years earlier.

Johnson stared at the image. Could this be their target? Johnson says, "It had many of the characteristics we were looking for. I was really excited but a bit guarded, as we had been disappointed before." Johnson bumped the image to the top of the list of coordinates to be investigated by their second ship, the *Argonaut*.

There was no more news during her watch. But afterward, when Johnson was brushing her teeth in her cabin near the ship's bridge, she heard a commotion outside. She hurried up to see what was going on. The captain of the *Flying Enterprise* had received a coded message from the *Argonaut*: The crew could stop current operations. Johnson's heart pounded. Had they found the vanished INS *Dakar*?

Missing: INS *Dakar* — Israeli submarine

Date last seen: January 25, 1968

Place last seen: Gibraltar

Possible reasons for disappearance:

sunk by enemy fire, collision,

mechanical failure

BACKGROUND

Just after midnight on January 25, 1968, the submarine INS *Dakar*, with a crew of sixty-nine men, was traveling at top speed through the eastern Mediterranean. It was on its way to Haifa, Israel, from Portsmouth, England. The crew had been reporting their position by radio to Haifa every twenty-four hours. Every six hours, they radioed a telegram, as well.

The sub was traveling quickly. In fact, it was on track to break a record for crossing the Mediterranean submerged. But after sending out a routine radio transmission at 12:01 P.M., the sub crew failed to communicate again.

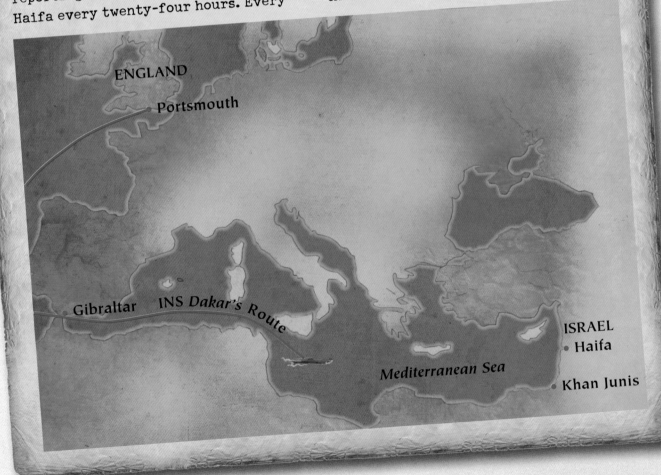

ENGLAND

Portsmouth

Gibraltar   INS *Dakar's* Route

Mediterranean Sea

ISRAEL
• Haifa

• Khan Junis

The next day, an international search mission was sent out. By sea and air, teams traced the *Dakar* route for any sign of the submarine. They found nothing. After two weeks, the search was called off. The *Dakar* had vanished, but the sub and its crew remained in the minds of the Israeli people.

Thirteen months passed without sign of the *Dakar*. Then the emergency buoy marker from the sub's stern appeared on the coast of Khan Junis, an Arab village, southwest of Gaza. When a submarine cannot surface, the crew may release buoy markers. The buoys remain attached to the submarine by a 180 m (600 ft.) metal cable. They float to the surface of the ocean and transmit an SOS message for forty-eight hours. Radio direction finders are then used to locate the downed submarine.

Experts examined the buoy and the small portion of cable attached to it. They determined that the buoy had remained attached to the *Dakar* for about a year before the cable had snapped. They believed the *Dakar* was close by and that she was between 50 and 70 nautical miles off her route.

Why had the submarine changed course, only to sink in shallow waters near Egypt? New searches were launched but to no avail. Had the ship been hit by an enemy weapon? Why couldn't anyone find it?

CASE OPEN

In 1997, twenty-five search missions later, a joint Israeli–American search committee entered the investigation, partnered with Nauticos, an ocean exploration company. They had new deep-water technologies, advanced satellite technologies and newly available information about Mediterranean currents. The team reasoned that the buoy could have been a misleading clue. They decided to return their attention to *Dakar's* original route.

On May 9, 1999, two ships, the *Flying Enterprise* and the *Argonaut*, arrived on site, and an intense naval search began. The tow ship, *Flying Enterprise*, began "deep-towing" a sonar device back and forth across the sea floor, much as a lawnmower cuts one swatch of grass and then the next as it moves across a lawn. The device took high-resolution sonar images of the ocean bottom in strips 2.5 km (2 mi.) wide.

The *Argonaut* stood by. It carried a remotely operated vehicle (ROV). The ROV was small, light — about 770 kg (1700 lbs) — and easy to maneuver. It was equipped with a video camera, a still camera and robotic manipulator arms, and could descend to about 6100 m (20 000 ft.). It also had forward-looking sonar to help it locate targets and get close enough to see them with cameras.

It was May 24 when Donna Johnson was shown the promising target. Says Johnson, "We contacted the *Argonaut* and gave them the coordinates so they could dive on it as soon as possible."

The ROV dove to 3000 m (10 000 ft.). It was guided to inspect the "special interest" site with its video camera. There, it discovered a 4 tonne (4 ton) section of a submarine's conning tower. This finlike compartment on the topside of a submarine contains the periscopes that direct the vessel.

Could a large freighter have collided with the sub and sunk it? One naval expert, viewing the wreckage, commented that the conning tower was quite distorted and torn, as if something, like a passing ship, had struck it a glancing blow.

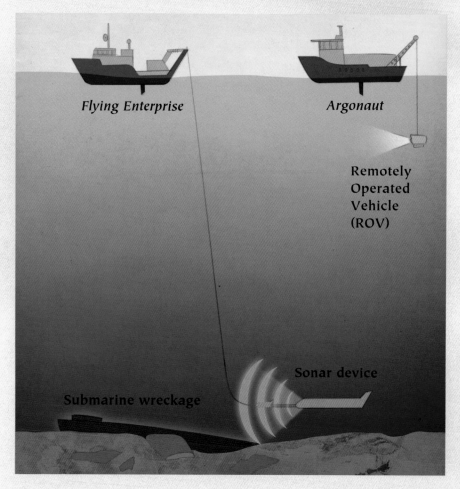

Flying Enterprise

Argonaut

Remotely Operated Vehicle (ROV)

Sonar device

Submarine wreckage

The ROV took photos and videos, and collected water and soil samples.

The ROV then discovered two large hull sections nearby. Its underwater camera revealed that the front section of the sub was intact, the middle section was damaged and the rear section had been slashed away. Inside the broken hull were objects such as periscopes, sonar domes and anchors. The camera also showed the bridge gyro repeater. It was lying face up, still showing the last course set by the submarine.

Naval experts rushed to the site and quickly identified the submarine — it was the *Dakar*.

Deep Sea Treasures

While searching in shallow waters for the *Dakar* in 1997, a research submarine photographed wrecks of two old ships. Further exploration revealed them to be early Phoenician merchant ships. About 2700 to 2800 years old, they are the oldest ships ever discovered in the deep sea!

The Dakar's *bridge gyro repeater*

The Dakar's *conning tower being raised.*

In 2000, the Nauticos team returned to the wreckage site. One of their goals was to look for human remains. There were none. The chemistry of the Mediterranean seawater had long erased any trace of the *Dakar's* crew.

The group's other goal was to raise the section of conning tower from a depth of 2900 m (9500 ft.). The team wanted to try to figure out what had sunk the Israeli sub.

There were many theories. Some still suspected enemy fire had downed the submarine. Tensions between neighboring countries had been high in January 1968, and many hostile vessels had been patrolling the area. Others believed that a large freighter might have collided with the *Dakar* and sunk the sub without realizing it. Yet another theory suggested that technical problems could have been at fault.

The investigation dismissed the first two theories. If the sub had been sunk by enemy fire, its pieces would have been scattered over a large area. High-tech imaging revealed that they were not. Neither was there any evidence of collision.

Investigators concluded that the sub had sunk because of flooding in the bow, which is the front of the ship. They knew this because the sub's bow was intact, even though it hit the sea floor. This showed that there must have been water inside, pushing against the hull at the same time that water outside the sub was pushing against the hull with equal pressure. When the bow hit the sea floor, it did not implode.

Investigators believe that severe flooding began in the sub's torpedo room, which is the most forward compartment. The weight of the water in the front of the sub would have caused it to plunge. The sub took on so much water so fast that the crew could not stop its rapid dive.

The hull, or body, of a submarine is made up of several watertight compartments. They are capable of withstanding the enormous pressure exerted by seawater at great depths.

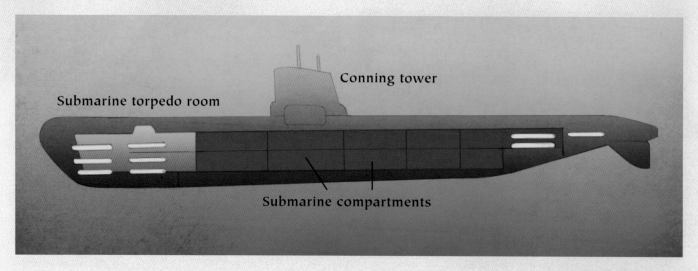

Conning tower

Submarine torpedo room

Submarine compartments

MYSTERY SOLVED?

If flooding in the bow left the *Dakar* in an uncontrolled dive, the sub would have been in grave danger. Nauticos president David Jourdan points out, "*Dakar* reached crush depth in barely more than a minute." A submarine can travel to great depths, but at a certain limit, the surrounding water pressure will crush its hull. For the *Dakar*, this limit was about 200 m (660 ft.). When it reached this depth, the sub's air-filled compartments imploded, "like a balloon bursting, but in reverse," explains Jourdan. "The force of the implosion was equivalent to about two tons of TNT ... It was a mess."

A monument honoring Dakar's sailors was built in the Mount Hertzel military cemetery in Jerusalem.

The INS *Dakar* has been found and officially identified. But, as David Jourdan says, "We will probably never know the exact cause of the flooding." Today, the recovered conning tower of the INS *Dakar* serves as a monument at a naval museum at Haifa, Israel.

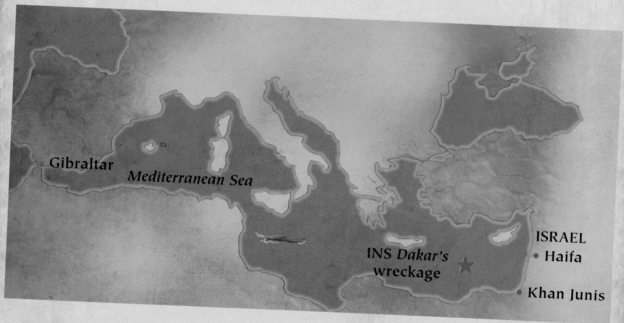

Gibraltar

Mediterranean Sea

INS *Dakar's* wreckage

ISRAEL
• Haifa

• Khan Junis

CASE CLOSED

... But what other factors might have played a role in flooding the submarine?

Glossary

anthropologist: an expert in anthropology, which is the study of the origin, behavior and development of humans

archaeologist: an expert in archaeology, which is the study of historic or prehistoric peoples and their cultures

artifact: any object made by humans

astronomer: an expert in astronomy, which is the study of matter in outer space, such as stars, planets and galaxies

chromosomes: the threadlike bundles of DNA and proteins, found in cells, that carry genes and pass along hereditary information

computer modeler: a person who creates computer programs that simulate how a system works in real life

computerized axial tomography (CAT): a type of medical exam in which a part of the body is scanned with X-rays. A computer combines the X-rays into a 3D image of the body part

core sample: a piece of material that is carved or drilled from a larger whole, such as wood from a tree or soil from the ground

data: a collection of facts from which we gain knowledge

dendrochronology: the study and dating of tree rings

DNA (deoxyribonucleic acid): a nucleic acid that carries the genetic information in the cell. DNA can be found in the nucleus and in mitochondria (where it is known as mitochrondrial DNA, or mtDNA)

electromagnetic radiation: waves of energy created by the movement of particles (the basic units of matter). Electromagnetic radiation includes radio waves, microwaves, infrared, visible light, ultraviolet light, X-rays and gamma rays.

evidence: something that provides proof

forensic anthropologist: an expert in anthropology and the study of the human skeleton whose knowledge is applied in legal cases, for example, identifying human remains

geographer: an expert in geography, which is the study of the earth, its features and life on the earth

glaciologist: an expert on glaciers, which are masses of ice that move across land

global positioning system (GPS): a navigation system that determines the location of a receiver anywhere on Earth by calculating how long it takes for signals from different satellites to reach it

historian: an expert on history, which is the study of events that occurred in the past

isotope: one of two or more atoms of the same chemical element (e.g., lead) which are similar but have a different mass

jet stream: high-speed winds that circle the globe at about 6 to 10 km (4 to 6 mi.) above Earth

magnetometer: an instrument used to measure the strength and direction of a magnetic field

naval engineer: a person responsible for the design, construction and/or repair of ships, boats and other sea vessels

navigator: the person onboard a ship or aircraft responsible for setting a course and steering the craft

orthodontics: a branch of dentistry that deals with how teeth line up and how jaws bite

orthophotograph: a special bird's-eye-view photo that shows distances as accurately as a map

radar: a system that pinpoints the location, direction or speed of objects by sending out electromagnetic waves and measuring how they are reflected from the surface of the objects

remotely operated vehicle (ROV): an underwater robot that is tied to a ship and controlled by someone on the ship

satellite: human-made equipment or a celestial body that orbits the Earth, the Moon or another celestial body

simulation: an imitation

social scientist: an expert in the study of human society and personal relationships

sonar: a system that finds underwater objects by sending out sound waves and measuring how they are reflected from the surface of the objects

spectroscopy: a way to identify substances by studying either the light, sound and particles they give off or those that they absorb

spectrum: the complete range of types of electromagnetic radiation

trace element analysis: the testing of a very small amount of material found within a sample, including both essential and toxic elements

wavelength: a measurement of light, heat or other energy

X-ray: a form of electromagnetic radiation that can pass through solid objects. X-rays are used in medicine to find bone fractures, cavities, tumors and foreign objects in the body.

Index